LOVE STRONGER THAN DEATH

Q. How many lives have you and Linda shared?

A. How many stars are in the sky? It's a never-ending song.

"The more I research psychic occurrences and explore human potential, the more aware I become of the unlimited power of love. Not only is its endurance assured throughout eternity, but the love bond seems fully capable of transcending time and space.

"Most of the people being regressed are experiencing it for the first time, and many I've worked with have had no belief in reincarnation. They don't know what to expect and wouldn't know how to fake the answers to my questions if they wanted to. . . ."

Books by Dick Sutphen

Past Lives, Future Loves
Unseen Influences
You Were Born Again to Be Together

Published by POCKET BOOKS

You Were Born Again to Be Together

by
Dick Sutphen

PUBLISHED BY POCKET BOOKS NEW YORK

A few of the names in this book have been changed in
cases where the subject would prefer to remain anonymous.

Another *Original* publication of POCKET BOOKS

POCKET BOOKS, a division of Simon & Schuster, Inc.
1230 Avenue of the Americas, New York, N.Y. 10020

Copyright © 1976 by Dick Sutphen

ISBN: 0-671-54151-X

First Pocket Books printing May, 1976

19 18 17 16 15 14 13 12 11 10

POCKET and colophon are registered trademarks
of Simon & Schuster, Inc.

Printed in the U.S.A.

SPECIAL THANKS

to all, both seen and unseen,
who helped on this book;

to Don Weldon for his spiritual
guidance, and for his words,
which I so often use;

to Trenna for her mental support
and physical toil.

With
peace, light, and love
to the
seekers of Truth

Preface

JOHNATHAN WELLS SLID HIS GOLD PAN INTO THE CREEK bed in search of placer deposits. He spun away when he heard the unmistakable sound of a rattlesnake in the brush beside him. The snake struck, sinking its fangs into his wrist. Johnathan reeled backward, grabbed a rock, and quickly killed the large diamondback. He then sat down and cut open the wound and began to extract the poison.

A short time later a young Yavapai Apache woman found him lying unconscious, his wrist swollen and bleeding from his own incisions. She immediately took the blankets from his bedroll, made him comfortable, and began to treat the wound. Repeatedly during the night she changed the poultice used to draw out the poison and maintained the fire to keep him warm.

The time was the late 1800s near Wickenburg, Arizona. It was summer and the hills were filled with prospectors and mine workers.

Johnathan recovered, and the Indian woman remained with him. Together, for the next several years, they worked the rivers and creeks of central Arizona, making a living but never much more. A daughter was born, and they settled down in the desert foothills in an adobe house they built. They had a small herd of cows.

Then late in the summer, seven years after they first met, they were panning in a creek near their home. A

flash flood from the mountains to the north rose as a wall
of water and almost instantly engulfed them. Johnathan
was able to swim to high ground, but he never saw his
wife again . . . until 1971, nearly one hundred years later,
when they met at a party in Los Angeles, California. She
was twenty-four and he was twenty-seven. They fell in
love at first sight and soon were married.

Today they own a small riding academy and horse
training center, living, working, and loving once more in
the foothills of Arizona.

They were born again to be together.

Contents

You Were Born Again
to Be Together

Love and Karma

LOVE IS THE MOST POWERFUL FORCE IN THE UNIVERSE. Not time, birth, death, or rebirth can finally separate those who have formed a deep mental, spiritual, or physical bond. The soul's affinity has been established, and those who know or have known love will always be "one."

Physical separation and parting for more than a short period of time, as we know it, is absolutely impossible. Mental separation is unknown on a subconscious level. Communication will always continue, although it may not be consciously perceived.

Lovers from the past will reincarnate within the same time frame again and again. Although they will not remember events of their past lives when they meet in their next life, they will be strongly attracted to each other, and love will be renewed.

In each new incarnation the love will deepen; hopefully it will grow more unselfish, until, after many lives, love is perfected.

People with whom you have a deep bond in this life have been close to you in a previous lifetime. You may have been lovers, friends, or relatives. The relationship could have been that of parent/child. But if you are intimately involved with another individual in your present life, the chances are great that you have been together in another time and in another place.

You were reborn to be with those you have known before. You were guided and maneuvered by unseen help from the other side, and by your own subconscious, intuitive, and extrasensory abilities to seek each other out again.

A colleague of mine was recently using hypnosis to regress a woman, and found that while in a deep trance state she was reliving an experience between lifetimes. She said, "I am watching the Masters plan a life." Further questioning explained what she saw. With the entity to be reborn, the Masters (highly evolved souls) were helping to plot the needed lessons for his life. This included his involvement with hundreds of other entities that would also be reborn within the same time, and the karmic interaction that would affect them all, offering each his needed opportunities. Astrology would be a factor. The exact moment and place of birth would set him on the proper path and would be a basic guide throughout his earth life. It was a job our finest computers would be incapable of attempting, but it is a part of the cycle of rebirth for every individual.

In every adult love relationship the initial attraction seems to be caused by physical and personal characteristics. But actually this attraction is the subconscious recognition of bonds created by a common past history. The fact is that you have known each other before, in some other lifetime.

Karmic history explains why you are so immediately attracted to some people, and also why you are repulsed by others. It accounts for the old adage, "Love is blind." Your meeting was predestined to occur as a classroom for your own soul's growth. Unknown subconscious forces within you welded the relationship and caused it to grow. You blocked the obvious negatives and saw only the positives. The faults you were able to perceive you felt you could change, handle, or overcome. If problems developed, they came later.

A completely untroubled relationship would provide no learning, so in most situations the unlearned lessons from the past begin to surface, to be worked out and ultimately balance the karma of all involved. Until you have learned from the past, you are destined to repeat your mistakes. <u>Learning is a process of remembering the past.</u>

Many people have extremely happy relationships which remain good. Love has been perfected. They have learned their past lessons and are here on earth for other growth experiences in this lifetime. They have earned the happiness they share by going through many traumatic lifetimes together, from which they gained wisdom and true love.

A couple from Tempe, Arizona, are a classic example. Regression showed that their initial contact with each other took place in fourth-century England. He had come from a North Sea coastal area as part of a Germanic war band that settled in England. She was a Saxon and a citizen of the Roman Empire which then controlled the country. The marauding band landed on English shores and began to pillage the countryside. The Saxon maiden was working in the fields when the Teutons invaded, and she was raped by the man who captured her.

For the next several months she was virtually a prisoner, used by the man for labor and pleasure. Although she tried desperately to escape, a strong love/hate relationship developed between captor and captive. Within the year the man was killed in a skirmish, and she was allowed to return to her own people.

A cycle had begun that has continued through four lifetimes that I know of. They may have lived many more lives than this, but we were able to re-create through regressive hypnotism the important incarnations in which they were drawn back together.

They next met as a Toltec man and woman in Mexico, but this time they both changed sexes and the roles were reversed. It was a relationship of male domination and cruelty, although from a karmic perspective it was a balance of the English lifetimes.

In their lives prior to their present existences, they returned to their original male/female roles on an Atlantic coastal island off southern Canada. They were married at a young age and made their living by fishing. The relationship was rocky and filled with conflict, but they raised three children and remained together until death at an old age.

They have now been married eleven years and remain in the same sexual roles. He is a career military officer, and she is a housewife. They have two children and a happy marriage. It took them four lifetimes together to achieve it.

In troubled relationships, regressive hypnosis often reveals why people have their particular problems. This knowledge, combined with the philosophy of metaphysics (the philosophy/religion/science of self in relationship to the universe-karma and reincarnation), provides a pathway to understanding and wisdom.

I recently regressed a Minneapolis man who was in Arizona on business. He had heard about my research through some mutual friends, and he was looking for the reasons behind his marital problems. He and his wife had been married for more than four years but had never developed a satisfying sexual relationship. He considered his wife frigid.

Regression showed an incarnation together as farmers in colonial America, each in their present-day roles. During a period of time while he was away from the farm, his wife had been badly molested and raped by three unknown men. The trauma of her personal experience was only magnified by her husband's attitude toward her from that time on. He could not accept what had happened and lost all physical interest in her.

She had carried into her present life not only the negative effects of the sexual experience but subconscious hostilities toward her husband because of his painful rejection in their prior life.

Ideally, through knowledge of the past causes, he will be able to show her his love through patience and understanding. Hopefully, she can rise above her hostility and sexual fears. They now have the choice of prolonging and perpetuating their karma, or together rising above it through love and wisdom.

While working with the Hypnosis Center experiment during 1973 in Scottsdale, Arizona, and since that time in private, college, and special group sessions, I have regressed thousands of people. Several hundred of these have been individual regressions. The most interesting have been investigated in detailed tape-recorded sessions. Often it has taken many sessions to complete the story of a particular lifetime. My own research has been primarily in man/woman relationships. In all my work in this area I have found only a few cases in which I have been unable to establish a past link between present lovers.

There is absolutely no doubt in my mind that men and women, together in this lifetime, have been together before. Even if their involvement is only a brief affair, there was a reason they needed to touch again. Today's situation could be explained by what happened yesterday. Or, to put it another way, because of "cause and effect," which is karma.

When you see an effect in the physical world, you can be sure that there has been a cause. If you throw a rock into a lake, it will send out ripples. The rock is the cause, the effect is the ripples, and you were another cause when you threw the rock. The river washed the rock down to the place where you found it. Before that a volcano erupted, forming the rock.

The chain of cause and effect would trace everything that has ever happened in the universe back to some original cause. When the effect is felt in man, the cause was set in motion in the mind. The effects you are feeling now, both positive and negative, are the results of causes from this lifetime or from previous lifetimes. The seeds (cause) you are sowing now will bring forth the effects yet to come in this lifetime or future lifetimes.

Your entire life—your mental state, your health, your relationships with others, the money you have or haven't made—all are effects, but somewhere in your background, in this life or in previous lives, these effects were set in motion by causes.

The law of karma works both ways—it rewards as well as punishes. I don't like the word "punish," for a negative event or crisis is not important from a metaphysical point of view. What is important is how you react to the crisis, how you think about what has happened. If you react in a positive way, you are erasing your karma. You have learned your past lesson. If you respond to the crisis in a negative way, with bitterness, remorse, revenge, or similar emotions, you have not learned your lesson, and sometime in your future you will once again have to come up against the "opportunity." When I say future, I mean this lifetime or lifetimes to come.

I know of a man whose wife seems hell-bent on undoing his mind. She has constant affairs, which she openly flaunts, and is fiscally irresponsible to the point of lunacy. On the surface he has every reason to be bitter and revengeful, yet to the best of my knowledge he has taken only logical steps to restrain her spending. He never condemns her in conversation and has tried in numerous ways to help her and better their relationship. To my way of thinking, he will never have to return within a similar environment, and will probably soon find an answer to his problem because he is responding with love and wisdom.

Everyone has many things to learn in a lifetime. We all come into this life with much intuitive understanding (the learning from our past lifetimes), which we will hopefully apply when the time comes, when the crisis develops. If we do, we have learned wisdom and we won't have to work on that lesson again. It will be time for new learning.

Karma is totally just. No one can argue that. It explains the supposed inequality we see around us daily. It explains sickness, health, affliction, fame, fortune, poverty, and life and death. As Kahlil Gibran said in *The Prophet*, ". . . the murdered is not unaccountable for his own murder." He meant that karma was being balanced.

Let's look at karma from the "reward" side. Take a man who has made a great deal of money . . . is this a reward, or is it a test? Did he make the money fairly, without hurting others or taking advantage of situations that in some way harmed others? Did he make it at the sacrifice of devoting some time to things that are more important than money? Is he using his resources beneficially or is he piling up negative karma on a personal power trip? He has been given his opportunity to grow in a special way. How he handles it will be balanced in the future.

If you've made mistakes in a personal relationship or marriage, you can use the time you have to learn from them. You do have the choice to rise above such negative karma—now.

I believe some marital relationships are destined to end, that the two individuals have learned all they can from each other in this life and that new opportunities are waiting for both.

If two people know it is over and feel divorce is the only answer, it is most important to achieve the parting without developing negative karma. Negative actions and emotions will produce negative karma. If this is the result, the two will have to go through it all again and probably with the same individual . . . in another life and in other bodies, until they've learned the lessons they set out to learn.

It seems that divorce, in some cases, is the primary reason for two people having come together in the first place. They have predetermined the situation as a test of their own soul's growth—to see if they have evolved to the point of parting under positive circumstances.

I completed eight regression sessions with a young divorcée who had recently moved to Phoenix from South Carolina. She was a perfect regression subject. She normally has a heavy southern accent, but while in a trance she speaks with an extremely crisp English accent. I carried her back in time through her former lives and even into a soul position prior to her first earth incarnation. She was then guided into the higher or superconscious area of her mind. I asked her to explain the divorce situation from this perspective. (Please realize that communication from this level is much different from communication in a regular regression—contact, when achieved, is established with the psychic, all-knowing mind.)

Q. Do you feel that you learned and advanced yourself through this marriage?
A. I have gained much knowledge, although I inflicted much pain.
Q. But do you feel you gained the desired understanding?
A. Yes.
Q. So this was a needed experience?
A. It was necessary, not looked forward to, but I realized the necessity.
Q. Were you aware of the outcome of this marriage before you were born?
A. Yes.
Q. Then the marriage was indeed structured and planned to start and end as it did?
A. Yes.
Q. Can you give me any understanding, since there was pain involved, why this was necessary?
A. It was regrettable that my husband was destined to experience the pain and disillusionment. It was necessary for me to experience living with one I did not love.

In the months that followed her divorce she had involvement with many men. At the time of the regressions she was in the process of forming a new relationship that for the first time in a long time seemed very important. I asked her about it.

Q. Can you give me any information about the reason you are so attracted to Bill?
A. It is not only a learning process for both, but it is also a reuniting of two entities, very much in love in a previous lifetime.
Q. Was this, too, destined before your birth?
A. Yes.

Shortly after this session she and Bill started living together. A year later they were married. That was two years ago, and from all outward evidence, although they have their share of worldly problems, they have a fine and fulfilling relationship.

A divorce involving negative actions and emotions will certainly create negative karma, but to remain unhappily married, turning your back on the situation by simply tolerating it with resentment and hostility, would also result in similar karma.

Karma is the universal law, and it guides unerringly. It will follow an entity through incarnation after incarnation until harmony is established between all effects and causes. A relationship involves two people—one may learn the lessons this time around, and one may not. Ideally the two people will get there together. You have the ability to achieve this wisdom by changing your ideas, thoughts, actions, and attitudes about others. If you learn this in this life, but your mate or lover doesn't, your mate will have to go through it all over again, but maybe next time it will be with someone else.

If you cannot remember what you have forgotten, you will be given another chance to learn. We are conditioned to respond to pain; instead we must learn to respond to love. Love is the force which energizes all growth.

Regressive Hypnosis

A WELL-KNOWN SOUTHWESTERN HYPNOTIST PUT ME into a deep trance and guided me backward in time . . . within minutes I was watching myself, almost like seeing a movie in my mind, running along a jungle path at the age of ten. It was me, but it wasn't. My skin was brown and I had black hair. I was wearing only a breechcloth, and as the pictures progressed I emerged into a village of structures such as I had never seen before.

The hypnotist carried me forward in time to the age of fifteen, and I was standing in a great plaza at sunset, the sun reflecting off the front of a huge temple. He asked me where I was, and I answered, "Copan." As he carried me forward, I watched myself grow up. As we moved through time, he asked me questions which I easily answered. Copan (Honduras) was the southernmost lowland Mayan site and was a cultural center of art and astronomy. It was the time of the Spanish conquest, and there was much fear and unrest among the people. The regression ended when I saw my own death in the midst of a conflict, as a Spanish soldier stabbed me in the back with a sword.

The last pictures I received were of myself lying in the arms of a woman, with a young boy standing close by . . . then they faded away.

Although I was lying on a couch in a comfortable office in Phoenix, Arizona, I was literally yelling, "They're tearing down our gods, they're tearing down our gods, we have no choice but to fight!" Tears were rolling down my cheeks, and I was trembling with emotion. The hypnotist then gave me strong instructions to calm down. While I was still in hypnosis, he carried me through death and into spirit and I was instructed to look back upon the Mayan life I had just come out of, to gain insight and understanding of the reasons for that life.

When awakened, I felt calm, but I was obviously shaken by the experience. Not only had I never heard of Copan, Honduras; I had virtually no historic knowledge of this time period. The only obvious surface link was my love of the statuary and art work of the Mayan people.

In the library I found books which substantiated several of the situations I had experienced in the trance. Geological records showed that the main temple in Copan did indeed face west, so the sun reflecting off the front was valid. The timing of events was correct, as were known facts about the activities of the people at this time. In the exact place I saw myself stabbed, I presently carry a light brown birthmark. It is thin and just about the width of a sword.

At the time of this first regression I was actively involved with self-hypnosis and a couple of metaphysical groups in the Phoenix/Scottsdale area. Reliving the Mayan lifetime was the beginning of several more regressions into other incarnations, and the beginning of a long study of hypnotism. I worked with established hypnotists and at first experimented with myself, using my knowledge of hetero-hypnosis, self-hypnosis, yoga, and metaphysics to work with trance levels and techniques to take myself into the past. This led to the combining of several hypnotic techniques with yoga techniques, and the experimental regressions of other people.

In 1971 I began group sessions with between fifteen and twenty-five people at a time. This experimental work resulted in the development of a technique that proved far more effective than any other I knew of. At least eighty per cent of those attending would go into a hypnotic trance.

I was told by everyone with any knowledge of the subject that there was no way to regress more than one person at a time. In a larger group one of the subjects could experience a traumatic situation that would require the hypnotist to calm him down or remove him from the trance immediately. This would cause everyone else to come back, too.

This objection was easily overcome by developing a "play it safe" regression, a technique which gives exact instructions for a self-release mechanism. The participants are also instructed to have their subconscious minds choose a lifetime in which they lived at least thirty years. They are told to re-experience only positive events which took place during that time. They are asked to see the situations in their mind and answer the questions to themselves which I requested. Before coming out of the trance, they are given a posthypnotic suggestion that they will remember every detail of everything they have experienced, and that they will continue to remember more and more about the previous lifetime after being awakened.

Through the group regressions it was easy to find the best subjects for individual regressions; I could then guide them through the past, asking questions and tape-recording the results.

As knowledge of the sessions spread, I started to work in colleges, schools, clubs, and with metaphysical groups. Regardless of the size of the assemblage, the results were always the same. The vast majority would re-experience a past life. While I did a group regression with a night class of forty-five people at Phoenix College, forty-two experienced past lives. Among the class members was a Superior Court judge and several civic leaders.

In 1973 the Hypnosis Center was established in Scottsdale, Arizona, as an intensified research project. For six months we worked with groups and individuals, taught classes and developed new regression techniques. Part of the Center program was an open session every Wednesday night, which always brought us new subjects. The most interesting cases were then followed up individually.

Often in individual regressions I will say nothing about past lives, but will explain to subjects while they are under hypnosis that the memory banks of their subconscious mind hold a memory of everything that has ever happened to them, every thought, every action and deed that has ever taken place. They are then asked to go back to the "very beginning" of the problems with their present mate. When instructed to tell me where they are and what they are doing, I have often found them in ancient times, reliving an experience of hundreds or thousands of years ago. I've even had subjects answer me in a foreign language.

A better understanding of man/woman relationships became the initial research work at the Center. Not only do we attempt to understand the lessons of the past but through hypnosis programming to alter the future. We developed rapid training methods to teach people to change themselves through self-hypnosis and thus alter the situations that surround their lives.

In January 1974 we closed the Hypnosis Center, but since that time I have continued to do research work, individually and with groups, primarily in the Phoenix and Prescott, Arizona, areas.

The case histories in this book are only a small percentage of those examined during the past four years. They are a word-for-word transcription of the tape recordings of actual hypnotic regressions, and in some cases the conversations prior to or following the sessions. The only variation, in a few cases, occurs where I have altered the order in which the information was obtained. It is sometimes necessary to move a subject backward and forward in time to gain a full understanding of a particular event or situation. Most of the material in this book is presented in its chronological context.

The first step in regression is to take the subject into a hypnotic trance. For this I use various methods that are dependent primarily upon the circumstances and the individual. The hypno-disc and the metronome, combined with yoga breathing and a too-warm room, are ideal for a subject who is to be hypnotized for the first time, but

unnecessary for the conditioned subject or the somnambulist. On one occasion I hypnotized an individual in a
crowded restaurant with vocal patterns and my ring.

Once in a hypnotic trance, the first-time subject is
usually taken back through his present life, a few years at
a time. Then detailed verbal instructions are given, taking
him back to a prior existence. If at that time visual impressions are not coming through, I have developed a unique
technique to start them flowing. It is this technique, which
I feel was directed from the higher realms, that has made
the regression of large groups possible.

It is important to realize that the cases in this book hit
only the highlights of an individual's prior incarnation.
We are skipping the mundane, everyday situations, searching out the events of importance that are burned into
the psyche. Often dates and similar data are hard to
acquire, simply because it wasn't important to the entity
back in his time. I have found this to be the case, more
often than not, in prehistory and medieval periods.

An entire past life is usually covered in from one to
three one-hour sessions. Often before awakening a subject, I will give him the following suggestions: "You will
remember everything you have received and re-experienced during this session, and you will continue to gain
more and more information about this past life as time
passes. This knowledge will filter down from your subconscious to your conscious mind in the form of thoughts
or visual impressions. If you consciously desire, your
dreams will also become a form of further enlightenment
with regard to your past life." In many cases this becomes
another information channel to clarify the experience.

In the case transcripts I will often describe the reactions
the subject is having to the past-life situation he is reliving. If it is traumatic, I will give him the strong suggestion "to look upon the situation only as an observer,
without pain and without emotion." The pain can always
be avoided, but the subject in regression fully realizes that
he is watching himself, or once again has become someone
from his own past, and it is often hard, no matter how

strong the suggestion, to prevent him from re-experiencing at least part of the emotion.

Often someone experiencing regressive hypnosis for the first time will feel that maybe his mind made up the pictures and data he received. I could make it more believable by instructing him, while under hypnosis, to block out all conscious memory of what he has just seen and re-experienced, then, once he has awakened, play the tape recording for him. But I do not believe in this, except in rare traumatic cases. Often much more is received by the subject than is encompassed within the verbal questions and answers. When the subject has been instructed to remember everything, I can usually obtain considerable additional information through talking with him after the regression experience.

In most cases where the subject has questioned what he received, I have heard later that something has happened in his life to substantiate the validity of the regression. Truth in metaphysics often has a way of surfacing to help show an initiate the pathway.

Recently I was instructing a golf pro in the techniques of self-hypnosis. She desired to lose weight and sharpen her concentration on the game. As part of the sessions we experimented with regression. She saw herself as a white child on a small Pacific island, waiting for a ship to pick her up. Her parents had died and she was being returned to civilization. The name of the island could not be verified at the time, but more than a year later she called to tell me she had been on a golf tour to Australia. On the return trip the boat stopped at an island that she instantly knew she had been on before; yet in her present life she'd never left the United States prior to that time. The island had once been known by the same name she had received in the regression.

The level or depth of a hypnotic trance can be easily tested if desired. While under hypnosis a subject can be regressed into his childhood to find information long forgotten by the conscious mind. He may refuse to answer a question, but if he does answer from a somnambulistic level, he will tell the truth. I know of no case where a subject in a deep trance has ever been able to lie. I believe the subconscious cannot stray from the truth when it moves from known reality into unknown past lifetimes.

Over the years the results of the regression have shown an absolute pattern. Most people being regressed are experiencing regression for the first time, and many I've worked with have had no belief in reincarnation, and no background in metaphysics. They do not know what to expect and would not know how to fake the answers to some of my key questions if they wanted to. Naturally, due to varying trance levels and other special considerations, there are some cases which I feel come through more clearly than others.

IMPORTANT NOTE:

If you are interested in experiencing past lives through hypnosis, I must strongly advise that under no conditions should you allow anyone other than an accredited hypnotist with a complete understanding of metaphysics to attempt the regression. There are preliminary spiritual "protection" techniques that should be implemented, through your guides and the use of white light. I always give a subject a self-releasing suggestion, and there are numerous other important considerations. The metaphysical understanding is necessary to comprehend many of the situations that are liable to come up, such as fear within the lower astral planes. Technical knowledge is necessary in cases of emergency. Often what seems a very positive suggestion on the part of the hypnotist will be received by the subconscious mind as a negative and must be quickly corrected.

Linda and Jim

"OH, MY GOD . . . NO, NO . . . HE WAS GOING TO KILL Ivan . . . I stabbed him . . . oh, God . . . the blood . . . the blood . . . no, no, no. . . ."

Linda was lying on the hypnosis couch, trembling with emotion, tears running down her cheeks. In her mind she was back in feudal England during a time of unrest and revolution and was reliving the moment when she had saved the life of her husband, who was almost killed by another man.

I first met Linda when she joined a self-hypnosis class I was teaching. She was just coming out of a very bad marriage and was under emotional strain.

About six months later we met again in a Phoenix restaurant. This time she was vibrant and happy. She explained that she was very much in love with a man she had known for some time but had only recently started dating.

The next time we saw each other, she came bouncing into my office. "How about regressing me sometime?" she asked. It had been well over a year since I had last talked to her.

"How about this afternoon?" I responded.

I knew from the class work that Linda was an extremely good, deep-level hypnosis subject. Before starting the regressions, we sat back for a cup of coffee.

"Tell me about your life now," I said.

"Well, I'm happy," she responded, "and I don't need self-hypnosis to try to convince myself that life is a positive trip. I still use it . . . but now only on things like relaxation and concentration. I met a very neat man about a year and a half ago. His name is Jim and we've been living together for sixteen months. We're going to be married in the fall."

"What does Jim do?"

"He works for a large sporting-goods company. Selling guns primarily. He'd like to get into writing and has done several articles lately for that underground paper that is put out by the college. He's very anti-establishment, I'm afraid. I'm always calming him down."

"What do you mean, anti-establishment?"

"Oh, the system, government, the way it is now. Things like the CIA. If there was any way to change it, he'd do it. I'm trying to convince him that changes take place through evolution, not revolution. That's why I'm glad he is writing—it's a way to get it out of his system. We're not Mormons, but he has joined a group—they're primarily Mormons. They get together every week and talk about survival and things like that. Kinda underground, I guess."

"Are you ready for a regression now?"

"I'm ready."

"All right, when you are under, I'm going to guide you into past ties with your present life, if indeed they do exist. O.K.?"

"Its a spooky idea, but I'm willing."

Linda

First Regression Session

July 1973

Hypnosis induced and regression preparation completed. The following instructions were then given:

You are presently in love with Jim. You plan to marry him soon. If you have ever known him before, at any time, in any place I want you now to return to the time of your first meeting. I will count from one to eleven, giving you instructions as I do so. On the count of eleven you will have moved backward in time to the time of your very first meeting with Jim, if you have actually known him before, in another time and another place. If you have not, on the count of eleven you will speak up and tell me so. (One to eleven count and instructions completed.)

Q. What do you see and what are you doing?
A. I'm riding . . . I'm riding with my maid . . . we're in the woods . . . it's bright and sunny.
Q. You're riding horses?
A. Yes.
Q. How old are you?
A. Eighteen.
Q. Tell me about the situation you find yourself in?
A. He's riding on a horse . . . he's stopping us.
Q. What does he say to you?
A. Well, we shouldn't be talking to him.
Q. Why not?
A. Because he is a peasant.
Q. What is he doing?

A. He's flirting with me. He has a beautiful horse . . . it's black and very well groomed . . . it's huge. He told me if I come back without my maid he'll let me ride it.

Q. Are you going to do that?

A. I shouldn't.

Q. If you do come back to meet him, I want you to move forward in time to that time. (Instructions given.)

Q. Did you come back to meet him?

A. Yes.

Q. How much time has elapsed since you first saw him?

A. Two days.

Q. What is happening now?

A. We're riding together and he is telling me of his work. He works with horses . . . smithing.

Q. Do you like him?

A. (Giggle.) He's terribly clever.

Q. Why do you say that?

A. He . . . ah . . . the court men are so boring.

Q. Tell me more about your conversation.

A. We're in a valley . . . it's green and it's . . . he's telling me that he lives by himself. His parents died.

Q. What is his name?

A. Ivan.

Q. What is your name?

A. Tilina.

Q. What country do you live in?

A. England.

Q. What year is it?

A. 1300 . . . 1370 . . . I think.

Q. Does Ivan live in a nearby village or town?

A. Just outside the village.

Q. Can you tell me the name of the village?

A. Salis. (Phonetic spelling.)

Q. Tell me about your own life. You mentioned you had a maid?

A. Well, yes . . . but she is more of a friend . . . a companion. She is my own age.

Q. Is your family wealthy?

A. Oh, yes.

Q. What does your father do?

A. He is a merchant.

Q. Does he live with your mother?

A. Yes.

Q. You mentioned the court, yet you say your father is a merchant. If he is a merchant, he is a working man—is that correct?

A. He is a very high . . . an important merchant.

Q. Then you do spend time with the people of the court?

A. Yes . . . but I don't enjoy it.

Q. All right, I am going to ask you some more questions about your relationship with Ivan. If there is anything of importance that takes place between the two of you romantically, or any other event of importance, I now want you to move forward in time to that time. (Instructions given.)

A. I'm at his cottage . . . I've been meeting him here. I want to stay with him . . . he's . . . oh, I love him . . . I want to . . . (Subject begins strong spinning sensations at this time, and stabilization instructions are given.)

Q. Are you deeply involved with Ivan at this time?

A. He wants me to marry him.

Q. Have you made love to him?

A. (Silence.)

Q. It's all right for you to tell me. I approve.

A. Oh, yes.

Q. What do you feel now?

A. I want to marry him, but my parents . . . they won't accept him.

Q. Have you discussed him with them?

A. No, if they knew we were meeting, they wouldn't allow it.

Q. All right, I want you to move forward in time again until something important transpires in your relationship with Ivan." (Instructions given.)

A. I'm happy but I'm crying . . . I'm . . . I have to tell my maid I'm leaving. She'll keep it a secret . . . but I have to go.

Q. Are you going to run away?

A. Yes.

Q. Move forward in time again to the time you meet Ivan to leave. (Instructions given.)

A. I'm handing him my bags.

Q. Where are you?

A. Outside the wall.

Q. Where are you putting the bags?

A. We're tying them onto the horses.

Q. Are you worried about being discovered?

A. No, it's dark.

Q. I want you now to move forward in time again to the next very important event that takes place in your relationship with Ivan. (Instructions given.)

A. (Subject begins heavy breathing, and she starts to moan and perspire; her face becomes very anguished.)

Q. (Strong suggestions given to see the situation only as an observer, without pain and without emotion.) I want you to speak up now and tell me about the situation you find yourself in.

A. (Moans continue.) I'm . . . I'm having a baby.

Q. Is there anyone there with you, helping you?

A. (Very slow response.) Ah . . . Ivan.

Q. Anyone else?

A. I don't think so.

Q. Where are you now?

A. In our house.

Q. Has the baby been born yet?

A. Oh . . . (Moans.) No.

Q. Move forward in time once again until the time the baby is born. (Instructions given.)

A. He's holding the baby . . . it's a girl. (Subject's voice patterns change completely at this time, becoming soft and gentle.)

Q. How are you doing now?

A. I'm so happy . . . I . . .

Q. Is there anyone else there with you now?

A. No, he helped me with the baby.

Q. Where do you live at this time?

A. In the forest, where we lived before.

Q. What has been your parents' reaction to what has happened?

A. I don't know. I haven't talked to them . . . over a year.

Q. What is the situation in England at this time? Is there peace, war, are the people satisfied with the government? Describe the environment in England at this time.

A. Ivan is . . . always talking about it. He's not happy about it.

Q. I want you to tell me about it.

A. He just . . . too much control . . . they take most of the people's crops . . . the lords and their men.

Q. Let's move forward in time to an important situation that arises in your relationship. (Instructions given.)

A. I know . . . Ivan's making something . . . he's in his shop . . . . I'm cooking and I can see that he is making something . . . he doesn't want me to go out there . . . It's for fighting . . . I know it's for fighting. . . .

Q. Is there fighting in your area at this time?

A. There is so much discontent between the peasants and the lords.

Q. (To establish time lapse.) How old is your daughter at this time?

A. Four.

Q. For the last four years have you, Ivan, and your daughter had a happy life together?

A. Oh, yes . . . I just . . . I want to be happy.

Q. You seem fearful at this time?

A. Yes . . . he's . . . he's just so angered.

Q. About the situation in England at this time?

A. Uh-huh.

Q. All right, let's move forward in time again to the next important situation that takes place. (Instructions given.)

A. (Subject becomes very anguished, breathing becomes deep, and her voice cracks.) He's going. (Calming instructions given.) Oh, he's . . . he made himself a metal chest plate . . . he's going . . . he's going to join a group. . . .

Q. Where are they located? Are they nearby?

A. No . . . it's a two-day journey.

Q. And you don't want him to go?

A. No. (Subject's voice is shaky, and tears appear on her cheeks.)

Q. Does he have to go, or does he feel he has to go?

A. He feels he has to go.

Q. What about the other men in your area—are they going?

A. Some of them . . . oh . . .

Q. Let's move forward in time again to the next important situation that takes place. (Instructions given.)

A. I took our little girl . . . I'm saying good-bye to her . . . I took her to our neighbor . . . woman . . . she's crying. . . .

Q What are you going to do now?

A. I'm going after him.

Q. What do you hope to do or achieve in going after him?

A. I've got to help him . . . I don't know . . . I just know I have to be there. . . . I have to be there . . . something tells me I have to be there. . . .

Q. All right, let's let go of this and move forward in time to the time you do meet or catch up with Ivan, if indeed you do. (Instructions given.)

A. Oh . . . I'm so tired . . . I've been riding . . . almost . . . so long . . . so tired. . . .

Q. Tell me the situation now—have you caught up with him?

A. I see a fire . . . I see a fire . . . it's Ivan's horse . . . there's someone else . . . someone else is riding.

Q. Where are they in position to you?

A. To the side.

Q. All right, describe the situation to me as it unfolds. Do you know this other rider?

A. No . . . I must be quiet . . . quiet . . . he's walking toward the fire. . . . (Panic in subject's voice. Long pause.)

Q. Is he walking openly toward the fire?

A. No, he's—oh, my God . . . oh, no . . . (Moans, panic

in voice; subject begins to tremble, and strong calming suggestions are given.) He was going to kill Ivan . . . I stabbed him . . . oh, God . . . the blood . . . the blood . . . no, no, no. . . .

Q. You stabbed the other rider?

A. I stabbed him . . . oh . . . he had a rock . . . he was going to hit him on the head. . . .

Q. Was Ivan sleeping?

A. Yes . . . oh, God, there's blood. . . .

Q. You were carrying your own knife then, and as this man crept up on Ivan, you came up behind him and stabbed him—is that correct?

A. Yes . . . oh, Ivan's holding me . . . I'm crying . . . God . . . oh . . .

Q. Remember now, you are only an observer looking at the past. Who was the man?

A. One of the lord's men.

Q. Had he been tracking Ivan down, or was this just a coincidence that he came across him?

A. I think it was just a coincidence . . . oh . . . (Subject is still emotional and breathing deeply.)

Q. Let's let go of this now and move forward to the next morning. (Instructions given.)

A. Ivan says he must go and meet the others. I can still feel the blood on my hands . . . I washed them but I still feel it.

Q. Did you kill the other man?

A. Yes.

Q. Are you going to go on with Ivan, or will you now return to your home?

A. No . . . he won't let me go by myself. . . . I'm going with Ivan.

Q. Let's move forward to the time you meet the other people. (Instructions given.)

A. We're talking with the others . . . they're all so . . . they're all so bloodthirsty.

Q. What do you want to do?

A. They want to fight . . . so mad . . . so long they have had everything taken from them . . . so mad.

The subject was obviously tired and emotionally distraught. Strong suggestions given for relaxation and mental peace. She was instructed to remember everything she had experienced and then was awakened.

(End of first session)

Although we had discussed the experience of regression in depth, Linda was unprepared for the actual encounter. She sat in the chair in total disbelief, slowly coming back to present-day reality. She looked at her hands, rubbing them. . . . "Me and my great ideas," were her first words to me. "How long was I under?"

"Altogether about forty minutes."

"I wish Jim were here . . . I feel so close to him now. I've never had a baby, but I have a feeling I just did . . . jeez. . . ."

"How do you feel now?"

"O.K., but I can't get it out of my mind. I thought I was going to throw up . . . when I saw . . . the blood, you know."

"We can go on with it if you like, but it would be best to wait a few days."

"Jeez, you can't stop now, teacher. It's like watching the first half of a movie that you're really into . . . I mean *really* into. If Jim and I were actually Ivan and Tilina, does that explain why we were so strongly attracted to each other? I guess I don't even have to ask that question. You know, he told me he used to have the same reaction to me when we used to see each other . . . before we were both divorced. I thought I had been in love before . . . with other people, but I know now . . . and I've known for some time . . . that I didn't even start to know real love before I met him. Wow!"

We discussed the regression further and then set a time a week later to follow up on the lives of Ivan and Tilina.

Linda

Second Regression Session

July 1973

(Returning to medieval England to the time of the meeting of the revolutionary group.)

Q. What do you see and what are you doing at this time?

A. We're in the woods. . . . Ivan's pacing. . . . It just seems they want revenge.

Q. Why do they want revenge?

A. They feel they have been robbed by the lords long enough.

Q. How have the lords been robbing them?

A. They make them work the fields, and then they come and take the crops, their men do.

Q. So what are you all going to do now?

A. They want Ivan to go with them . . . he's just . . . he's torn . . . . He wants to fight, yet he knows how useless it is . . . too.

Q. Are there many of you?

A. From the different villages . . . there are only about twenty here now.

Q. Let's move forward in time a couple of days. (Instructions given.)

A. Ivan and I are riding together . . . we're just talking. . . . He's trying to explain to me . . . how he knows the others expect him to go. . . . He'd really rather come back with me . . . but the others expect him there.

Q. Let's move forward in time to a situation where something very important takes place. (Instructions given.)

A. I won't go back! I'm going with him. (Determined voice.) I won't actually fight, but I can disguise myself.

Q. Move forward to an actual confrontation, a fight, if indeed this does transpire. (Instructions given.)

A. I'm dressed up . . . well . . . I'm dressed up like I used to be. . . . I'm dressed in very fine clothes . . . silks.

Q. What is the situation then?

A. I'm laughing and talking with one of the coachmen . . . and I . . . told him that I just wandered away . . . wandered away too far from the court . . . and he's flirting with me. . . .

Q. Why are you doing this?

A. The men are going to attack . . . the coach is stopped . . . the . . . the coach is filled with three men . . . they are very finely dressed. . . . They got out and they are kissing my hand. . . . They are offering me a ride to the court. . . . OH, GOD . . . I've got to get out of here . . . oh, my God.

Q. Tell me what is happening?

A. The men . . . they've attacked . . . the driver is hit with an arrow . . . he fell off the coach . . . he's choking. . . . I'm running . . . I'm running through the woods . . . I'm running . . . running."

Q. Were you a decoy, then, to stop the coach?

A. Yes.

Q. What are the men doing now?

A. Killing . . . they are taking their jewels off their fingers . . . they're searching through their bags . . . killed . . . every one. . . . We're supposed to go back to the horses.

Q. What was the purpose of all this?

A. The coach carried officials . . . higher lords. . . . We are trying to anger them enough to draw them out to us . . . instead of us attacking the walls.

Q. All right, let's move forward in time again just a few hours. (Instructions given.)

A. Ivan and I are lying by the fire . . . he's trying to tell me how good I was today. . . . I just feel such a frustration . . . I just want to be home with him and our daughter . . . but yet . . . he's telling me I'm important . . . important to them. . . . I will stay with him . . . I have to. . . . Ivan can't take me back, I can't go alone—it's too dangerous.

Q. Let's move forward in time to the next time you confront the enemy. (Instructions given.)

A. They're all in the trees . . . there is supposed to be a group of soldiers coming back. . . . We will attack . . . I am supposed to warn them . . . that they're coming. . . . I am to shoot an arrow. . . . I hear them . . . I hear them coming . . . I don't . . . I just feel . . . my heart is just beating so fast. . . . (Subject shows anguish and strain; her voice is scared.) I can see them . . . they're riding by me. . . . I shot the arrow . . . now I can see them . . . down below the men are jumping from the trees . . . knocking the men off their horses. . . . Oh, Ivan . . . Ivan . . . oh . . . oh, I just . . .

Q. Tell me about the situation as it unfolds.

A. Why does it have to be done this way? (Subject's voice is scared and frustrated.) The enemy is dead . . . some of our men hurt . . . the wounds . . . oh . . . (Tape is hard to hear here; subject almost seems to be talking to herself.)

Q. Who were the men who were killed?

A. The lord's men . . . soldiers.

Q. What will you do now?

A. We'll go back to the camp . . . the men will celebrate.

Q. Let's move forward in time again, to a time when a new situation develops. I'll let the memory banks of your subconscious mind choose the situation. (Instructions given.)

A. We're sitting around the fire . . . the men are all talking . . . they're planning to organize . . . to organize the villages and more men in order to storm the walls.

Q. If this does happen, let's move forward in time to the time this situation takes place. (Instructions given.)

A. I'm sitting on the horse beside Ivan . . . we're talking. . . . There are hundreds of men . . . we're all hiding . . . we're waiting for the proper time. . . . I'm dressed in leather. . . . I'm so afraid Ivan will be killed . . . they have broken through . . . when the gates were open . . . there is fire . . . fire everywhere. . . .

Q. Where are you right now?

A. Ivan is fighting . . . I'm supposed to do something . . . what is it . . . I don't know . . . supposed to . . . (Subject's voice is afraid and confused.)

Q. Move forward in time to the end of the battle. (Instructions given.)

A. Oh . . . oh . . . oh . . . (Subject is talking so low that she can't be heard. To herself again.)

Q. What are you both going to do now?

A. We're going home . . . home to our daughter.

Q. How many days' journey will this be?

A. At least another two or three.

Q. Is Ivan able to travel?

A. Yes, uh-huh.

Q. All right, let's move forward in time to the time you do get back home, if indeed this does happen. (Instructions given.)

A. Oh . . . oh, our home is . . . it's been ripped apart . . . terrible. . . . The soldiers have been using it . . . everything . . . everything is strewn . . . dirty. . . .

Q. What about your daughter—is she all right?

A. We have to go get her . . . she's at the house where . . .

Q. Move forward in time to the time you go to get your daughter. (Instructions given.)

A. Ivan's holding her . . . it's so good to see her . . . she's grown so much.

Q. Does she recognize you?

A. Yes . . . oh, yes . . . it's so good to hold her.

Q. What is the situation around your home? Is there fighting in your area now?

A. There was, but not now.

Q. Who is winning?

A. I don't know . . . the fighting just seems to go on forever . . . we hear things weeks after they have happened.

Q. Tell me what you see.

A. Dead people . . . dead people are everywhere . . . I don't want to see it . . . just don't want to see it . . . dizzy . . . so dizzy. I'm on the ground. (I believe Tilina fainted at this point, for there is a blank time of no response.)

Q. Tell me what's happening now.

A. The men who are left are raiding the houses. . . . Where is Ivan . . . Ivan. . . . I think the soldiers are coming . . . we have to leave . . . we have to leave. . . . Oh, I'm so dizzy. . . . I'm trying to see . . . oh, he's hurt . . . oh, God . . . his arm . . . his shoulder. . . . Oh, God . . . I'm helping him . . . I'm holding him . . . we're stumbling out . . . get to the woods. . . . Oh, please, Ivan . . . please . . . please . . .

Q. What is it you want him to do?

A. I want him to go home . . . our daughter is six . . . he's ready . . . ready . . .

Q. He's ready to go home with you?

A. Yes.

Q. How badly is he hurt?

A. Not too badly . . . I don't think . . . his arm. . . . He's riding . . . I helped him on the horse . . . he's drooped over the horse . . . we're leaving.

Q. Let's move forward in time two days. (Instructions given.)

A. We're in a cottage . . . it's . . . the people are helping Ivan . . . . I'm eating some of the old woman's broth.

Q. How is Ivan doing at this time?

A. All right . . . the old woman . . . she boiled the bark . . . and put it on the wounds . . . then wrapped his arm in cloth. . . . He's eating the broth.

Q. What will you and Ivan do now?

A. Don't know . . . I feel we're just going to try to protect our home. . . . He is still concerned . . . he's going to try to . . . uh . . . he talks about helping the men by forging weapons . . . I think the swords kept on breaking . . . he wants to experiment with explosives. . . .

Q. Let's move forward in time two years. (Instructions given.)

A. Ivan has made many . . . he has hidden storage places . . . swords. . . . If the soldiers come by, it looks like he is working on the horses . . . but most of the time is working on . . .

Q. There is still unrest and revolution in the country then?

A. Yes . . . the soldiers leave us alone . . . they don't know what we do . . . and . . . uh . . . we . . . uh . . . we feed them when they come by . . .

Q. Do your own men then come to get the material Ivan forges?

A. Yes. . . . They come at night . . . they understand what we do.

Q. All right, let's move forward in time again to the next very important situation that takes place. (Instructions given.)

A. I don't want to . . . I don't want to see it . . . we've been so happy . . . I don't want to.

Q. You have the power and ability to look at this only as an observer, without pain and without emotion. I now want you to speak up and tell me about the situation you find yourself in.

A. Ivan has been pounding in the . . . (Voice trails away.) I'm looking across to his shop. . . . The soldiers rode up . . . my daughter is hiding behind me. . . . They're so angry . . . so very angry. . . . They've found out what we do . . . I'm trying to explain to them that we are loyal . . . loyal to the lords . . . we just shoe horses. . . . They're not believing me . . . (Voice is starting to panic.) oh . . . uh . . .

Q. Without pain and emotion, I want you to explain to me what is happening.

A. I grabbed my daughter . . . they've shot me . . . an arrow . . . they've shot me. . . . Ivan sees what's happening . . . he didn't hear . . . he's running to me. . . . I'm lying on the ground—go back in . . . run, get away. . . . No, no, running to me . . . uh . . . (Subject stops talking.)

Q. If you were killed at this time by the arrow, I now

want you to cross over into spirit, leaving your earthly body without pain. You will be able to talk to me and answer questions from the spirit level. (Instructions given.) Tell me what you see and what you are experiencing now.

A. We were so young.

Q. Can you see your own body?

A. Yes . . . but I seem to be floating. . . . They're throwing us over the horses.

Q. Was Ivan killed too?

A. Yes.

Q. Can you see your daughter?

A. She ran to the neighbor's house where she stayed . . . she is so scared. . . . I always told her to run . . . if the soldiers ever came and were mean, I told her to run like she never ran before.

Q. Where were you hit with the arrow?

A. The back . . . I turned to grab my daughter and it hit me.

Q. What is happening now?

A. The soldiers are talking about using the bodies to make an example of us.

Q. Is Ivan there with you in spirit?

A. Yes . . . oh, yes . . . oh, yes.

(Instructions given to return to the present, calm and relaxed and filled with peace. Subject awakened.)

"Welcome back to 1973, Linda."

"Wow! . . . I mean wow! It's going to take quite a while to absorb all that—wow!"

"How do you feel?

"Fine . . . I think. . . . That being dead part was really weird. It was like I didn't feel anything—I was just floating, watching what was going on. I think I understand why I try so hard to calm down Jim's revolutionary ideas. Once is enough."

"Are there any other ties between this life and the life in England that you can think of?"

"Well, we both love to ride, but of course that's rather natural, living in Arizona. We've talked about getting our own place, hopefully out north of Scottsdale where we can have our own horses. Jim has a collection of hunting knives, and one big bowie knife. He has them mounted on the wall in the living room. There again, though, a lot of people in Arizona do that sort of thing. I'll tell you one thing, though . . . if he starts to do any blacksmithing he's gonna be in bad trouble."

"Would you be interested in doing one more session, only this time we will search for past ties with your first husband?"

"Sure . . . what could be worse than being shot with an arrow?"

(End of second session)

FOLLOW-UP NOTES:

Linda consciously knew nothing of medieval England, yet a study of the time period covered in the regressions (approximately 1370 to 1381) produced the following historical facts:

The members of the merchant guilds were among the wealthiest and most privileged people in England during this time. They guarded their traditional control of urban economic life and ruled as narrow oligarchies over the towns.

The longbow was developed during the reign of Edward I (1272–1307).

Both Edward II and Edward III were the kings of England during the regression period. This was a time of political and social conflict. Royal taxation was intensified, and the subjects of the realm were sullen and rebellious. A general atmosphere of unrest was prevalent throughout the country, with numerous small rebellions taking place.

During this time the majority of the peasant population was held in a state of bondage to the lords. To farm the land, the peasants were required to contribute a percentage of their labor, or crops, or both.

This was the exact time the local lords were assembling permanent private armies. These private military retinues often terrorized the countryside, bringing about a breakdown of local government and an epidemic of local warfare. The justices of the peace did their best to keep order in their districts, but frequently they were unable to cope with the private armies of powerful local lords.

Gunpowder was being developed and experimented with in England during this time.

The local fighting finally erupted in May 1381, into what is labeled in history "The Peasants' Revolt." This massive, bloody uprising was the final result of the conflict between the lords and their tenants. After terrorizing the lords and gentry of England, the bands merged and marched on London, and by mid-June the city was in chaos. The court took refuge in the Tower, and the Archbishop of Canterbury was captured and killed. Although deeply hostile to the lords, the rebels remained respectful of the monarchy. They sought the abolition of villenage—the freeing of all peasants from the traditional work service on their lord's lands. Although the king momentarily submitted to their demands, the end result was that the rebel bands were hunted down and the old social order restored.

Linda

Third Regression Session

August 1973

In this session we moved back in time to find a past tie with Linda's first husband. When the regression count was completed and I asked her, "What do you see and what are you doing?", she was confused and was receiving two distinctively different mental pictures. One was of a girl in an American 1920s style dress, leaning over a piano, talking to the piano player. The other was of a native girl standing on a beach talking with a man. (This probably signified two prior lifetimes in which they knew each other.) The native impressions took over, and she saw herself talking with an old man. "He is looking very sternly into my eyes," she said. "I have to do what I am expected to do. . . . I have to marry the man who won me."

As we moved through a lengthy regression session, the following facts became known. She was a female of marriageable age, living on an island "one day's journey" in length. The man she was to marry was strong and more feared than respected by other members of the community. Her wedding night experience proved to be more like rape than lovemaking. For two days following the experience, she lay in their hut, bleeding vaginally. Bad feelings developed between her own family and her new husband, and with the passage of time she grew more and more despondent about her marital situation. "Death is my only release . . . I just want to die," she said.

A friendship with a male member of the group was interpreted by her husband as an unfaithful act. "He's lying to everyone, he's telling them I have been unfaithful . . . that I was going to leave with the other man. . . . We were seen together, and he's lying to everyone. . . . He's disgracing me in front of my people." (Subject shows extremely strong emotion.)

Q. Do your people believe him?
A. Yes . . . I think he actually believes it is true.
Q. What is happening now?
A. He's dragging me . . . he's dragging me . . . he's thrown me down in front of the old man . . . he is sad . . . he looks at me so. . . . Once when I was a small girl, he saw me drowning—he sent one of his boys out to save me . . . and we've always been . . .

close . . . because of that. . . . He has tears in his eyes . . . he knows he can't make an exception . . . oh . . . oh . . .

Q. What is the punishment for being unfaithful?
A. I will be killed.

Strong suggestions were necessary to calm the subject down. I carried her forward in time to the execution of her punishment. She saw herself being savagely carried up a mountain pathway by several men. At this point the subject tried to block out the mental images, refusing to re-experience the situation. Her last words were, "Falling . . . falling."

"All right, you are now letting go of this experience. I am now going to carry you into the higher levels of your mind. You will rise into the superconscious God level of your own mind, the all-knowing level of your own mind, and from this perspective you will be able to answer any questions I ask of you." (Instructions given.)

Q. I want you to tell me now how you were killed in the island lifetime we have just been examining.
A. (Totally different voice pattern.) I was thrown into a volcanic crater.
Q. Was your husband in the island lifetime Tom, the same man you were previously married to in your present incarnation?
A. Yes.
Q. Have you known him in any other lifetimes?
A. Yes.
Q. Were the first images you received of a woman in 1920s-style dress from a lifetime in which you were also together?
A. Yes.
Q. Can you explain to me the basic situation between the two of you in that life?
A. He was very much in love with me, but I left him to marry a wealthy man.

(End of third session)

"Jeez . . . Jeez . . . that was my nightmare. I've had that nightmare all my life. My father used to have to come in and wake me up . . . he'd almost have to slap me to bring me out of it."

Linda was wide-eyed, sitting in the hypnosis chair, shaking her head. "My sister could tell you about it. She used to have to sleep in the same room with me . . . wow!"

"Tell me about it," I said.

"Well, every six months or so I'd have it. I used to pray that I wouldn't have it any more. It was always the same . . . I'd see these men carrying me up a hill, and I was struggling . . . kicking, you know . . . and then they'd throw me into a huge hole. My dad said he couldn't believe how I'd be thrashing about when he tried to wake me up. I don't think I've had the dream now for maybe five or six years."

"I doubt, now that you know the whole story, that you'll ever have it again," I told her.

"I think I liked being shot by the arrow better."

FOLLOW-UP NOTES:

An obvious karmic assessment, based upon the limited knowledge received through the regression, would be that Linda and her first husband (Tom) were reborn in the 1920s, and in that incarnation Linda walked out on him, due to the subconscious hostilities she was still carrying from the island lifetime. The fact that she married another man for money may have established a guilt, or debt with Tom, in her own mind.

In this lifetime she quit school to work, to put him through college. After he was established in his profession, it was the cash values of her own childhood insurance policy that provided the down payment on their home.

Throughout their marriage Tom had been dictatorial and violent, often hitting Linda. One such incident is carried in the local police files. Shortly after they were established in their house, Linda made the decision to leave. Tom was given the house, the family car, and the majority of their possessions. Linda probably felt sub-consciously at this time that the old debt had been repaid.

By the time we had finished discussing the regression it was the end of the day. Linda was going to meet Jim for a drink at the Bombay Bicycle Club in Scottsdale, and she asked me to join them. I agreed.

Jim was a tall man, wearing a western-cut coat and Levi's. His hair was long, coming not quite to his shoulders. We exchanged the usual amenities, and the three of us sat down at a corner table. "I've just taken your fiancée on another wild trip, I'm afraid."

"She's been calling me Ivan ever since the last one," he responded. We all discussed the latest regression for the next few minutes.

It was obvious that Linda and Jim were very much in love. "I've been thinking about the Ivan lifetime," Jim said. "Ever since I was in about the eighth grade, I suppose, I've made sketches of unusual weapons that I have designed. I've never actually constructed any of them, but I have a huge file folder full of every conceivable kind of fighting device. I designed and worked out a pattern for throwing knife stars in high school. That was quite a few years before they became popular on *Kung Fu.* Another thing that might tie in . . . I've always been super-interested in English history. It is certainly nothing that I ever discussed with Linda, but back in school it had much more fascination for me than the history of any other country, even our own."

"I understand Linda would like to suppress your revo-lutionary tendencies."

"No matter how much I love him, I've explained that I'm not acting as a decoy for any fancy coaches this time around. I guess I'll help him write his articles, as long as he hires someone else to shoe our horses."

We ended the conversation, talking about the plans for their coming wedding and their future life together.

(Follow-up—June 1975)

Linda and Jim have now been married for more than a year and a half. I called them recently while I was in

Scottsdale on business. "Come on out and have a drink with us," Linda bubbled over the telephone, and then gave me instructions on how to find their place. They live fifteen miles out in the desert, in the northernmost part of the Phoenix valley. As I pulled into their driveway I drove past a corral in which two well-groomed quarter horses stood under the sun shield. A very pregnant Linda greeted me from the front porch. "Welcome, stranger. Haven't seen you since the wedding," she said as she patted her stomach. "Been a few changes since then."

"You swallowed a watermelon?"

"No, just the seed . . . it's taken about eight months to get to this point. Not much sunshine can get in, you know."

"You're happy."

"Yeah, I really am . . . no complaints."

We went inside. Jim wasn't home from work yet, and Linda went into the kitchen to fix a couple of drinks. Their house was hardly pretentious, but it was clean and comfortable, standing on ten acres of their own land. Jim was constructing a small barn adjacent to the corral.

"What do you think?' she asked, returning with a tall glass of welcome relief from the 107-degree afternoon.

"Looks just like what you'd hoped to put together. I dig it."

"We're working on the barn together. Hope to have it done by the end of the summer. Of course I'm not too much value at the moment, but I can hold nails good."

We talked about their present life together. Linda had quit her job shortly after their marriage. Jim was now selling sporting goods as an independent rep, and Linda devoted a good part of her days to keeping the books, handling the invoicing and related business chores. They obviously worked easily and well together. Jim no longer attended the underground meetings, although he continued to work at getting his writings published.

"He's mellowed a bit since you last saw him. Not that he has changed his thinking, but he's concentrating more energy into developing our place as a survival center.

We have a lot of dehydrated foods, wheat and things like that. When the barn is done, we'll put in our own generating system. If we could afford to totally drop out, we would. Maybe someday."

"Do you get along well?"

"Oh, yeah, wow! I can't believe how neat it is. We've had a few little fights, I guess, but they're never about anything important, and we both get over them instantly. He says I support him, and I guess I do. Anyway it comes natural."

As I was climbing into my pickup to leave, Jim pulled in. We talked for a few minutes. He puts his arms around Linda, rubbing her stomach. "I'm not delivering this one," he said.

Sharon and David

"I HAVEN'T SEEN HER FOR SIX YEARS, BUT THERE IS never a day goes by that she doesn't at least come into my mind."

David and I sat talking about a former love he had never really gotten over.

"Do you know what's happened to her in that time?" I asked.

"We've talked on the phone several times . . . the last time was about a year ago. She's married now and has a two-year-old son," he responded.

David had married five years before and has a four-year-old daughter, in addition to children from his first marriage. His relationship with his present wife, although spirited, is basically happy.

"I don't know why I still think about her so much. Maybe because we both wanted so bad for it to work out, and it didn't. When we have talked, we both know the old feelings are still there—under the surface, I mean —we just know that we're on different tracks now. Our life-styles would be as far apart now as the miles that separate us. She still lives back in Minnesota. I'd sure like to believe your way of thinking . . . that we've been together before, and that maybe sometime in a future life we'll have a chance to be together again. What about after death—do you believe that real lovers are rejoined?"

"I do. I feel we were reborn within the same time

frame for the specific purpose of being together in the physical body . . . to work on needed learning together. This often goes beyond just a few important individuals. Whole groups or tribes will sometimes incarnate together. I personally know, 'my truth,' that I'm part of a group that goes back at least to ancient Mexico. We've all been reunited in the southwest, and much of the interaction among those close to me is related to past ties."

"Make me a believer," he said jokingly, but in all seriousness.

"There's a lot of reading you can do. We can try a regression if you'd like, but I'd prefer to give you some conditioning first."

On directed individual regressions, unless a subject has been previously hypnotized, knows self-hypnosis or yoga, I will, ideally, personally condition him for the experience, or use cassette tapes that allow him to prepare himself. In David's case I gave him some self-hypnosis tapes and explained how to use them. Two weeks later we met again.

"Tell me about the situation with the woman in your past."

David was sitting across from me, sipping a cup of hot coffee. He was relaxed and easy in his conversation.

"I've been thinking a lot about it, knowing that we were going to be doing the regression and all. It certainly isn't that I don't love my wife—we really have a neat thing going between us.

"I know that if I had the chance to get back together with Sharon tomorrow, I wouldn't take it . . . I wouldn't be able to give up what I now have. Yet, as we talked about it before, Sharon is always in my mind. It isn't like it used to be. A few years ago my stomach would do a flip-flop every time I saw a car like the one she used to drive. I used to project her reactions into all the little everyday situations that came up in my life. I was really hung up, I guess."

David continued, "It was six, almost seven years ago now. I had a small commercial art studio in Minneapolis —my background was working as an art director in advertising agencies, and I had been on my own for a little over a year. Business was booming, and I hired another artist and a rep. My wife and I had been handling the bookkeeping and secretarial chores, but it was getting to be too time-consuming . . . plus we needed a receptionist in the studio. So I started looking for a girl to fill the position. A friend told me about a local company that was closing out its business and the name of a secretary/receptionist who would soon be needing a job. I stopped in to talk to her and was literally floored by my reaction. She was beautiful, but it was more than that . . . I've never been so attracted to anyone in my life. We talked and she was interested in the position. We set a time, a couple of days later, for her to come by the studio to discuss it further. Hell, I would have hired her even if she couldn't type.

"At that time I had been married for seven years. We had kids. There were frustrations in our relationship, but I had never been unfaithful in all those years. Yet for the next two days I thought about nothing but Sharon. When she came to the studio, we agreed upon the duties of the position and the salary. The same attraction was there, stronger than ever. That was in April. By July I was so much in love with her it hurt. Until then nothing had happened between us. We spent hours talking and usually ate lunch together. Then one day when we were working alone, I kissed her. She responded . . . I mean she really responded. She had been feeling the same thing, the same frustrations I had. After work we went to a small bar and talked very openly. She was also married—had been for about two years at that time, I believe. Her marital relationship had gone downhill since the day we first met. She explained that she had wanted almost no physical involvement with her husband since then. The next day was Saturday—I met her early in the morning and we drove to a motel in a nearby town."

"From then on we were together every minute we could beg, borrow, or steal. We couldn't get enough of each other in bed. I never knew sex could be so beautiful. But I was new to this sort of thing, and I wasn't handling it well at home. My wife knew something was very wrong, and finally one night when she was really pushing me about what it was, I broke down and told her the whole story. She didn't handle it well at all, and we started a series of on-again, off-again separations. Sharon left the studio, but we couldn't stay away from each other, which certainly wasn't helping either of our marriages.

"Then about November my wife took the kids and left the state. I was really torn up then . . . finally making the decision to go after her and try to put it back together. I'll never forget how Sharon cried, she wanted me to take her away . . . she wanted to leave with me . . . to go anywhere and start a life together. I was so filled with guilt I couldn't do it. I followed my wife to Arizona and we tried to put it back together, but it didn't work.

"Several weeks later I returned to Minneapolis. My business was really suffering by then. Sharon met me at the airport and we started seeing each other again as much as possible, but by this time her parents and husband were aware of the situation and the weight really started to come down. It was a time of the 'crazys'— guilt so deep you couldn't see over it. Her mother and father were on her back all the time, and her husband was going through hell. Yet we kept seeing each other . . . sneaking around . . . I wanted her to leave, to go someplace else and start fresh, together. But she had so much pressure on her, from so many areas, she couldn't let go. Finally in April I couldn't handle it any more and decided to move. I'd always loved Arizona, so it was my choice. I wanted her to come with me, but she couldn't.

"For the next year we stayed in contact on the phone, and we got together in motel rooms when I traveled back to Minnesota on business every month or so. She was holding her marriage together somehow. God, I wanted her to come to Arizona, but nothing happened. Then I met a girl down here, my present wife, and we started seeing a lot of each other. Minnesota business had dwindled by then and I had no excuse to be commuting back and forth. That next July I married my wife. The saddest part of it all was the following month Sharon and her husband were divorced. She came to Arizona, but by then I was committed. She used to call me after that from Minnesota, every once in a while. Once during a time when my wife and I were really having a hard time . . . I'd probably have gone back to Sharon, but my wife was pregnant by then. It really seems like we just weren't meant, or weren't allowed to get it together this time around."

David

First Regression Session

January 1975

Hypnosis induced and regression preparation completed. The following instructions were then given: "You have known and loved Sharon in your present lifetime. If in fact you have known her before, in another time and another place, we are now going to return to that past lifetime. On the count of eleven you will see yourselves together once again. If you have not known her before, on the count of eleven you will speak up and tell me so." One to eleven count and instructions completed.

Q. What do you see and what are you doing?
A. We're walking in a flat grassy area above the river.
Q. Who is walking with you?
A. Margaret . . . my wife.
Q. What is your name?
A. Samuel.
Q. How are you both dressed?
A. Margaret is wearing a long white dress. . . . I have on a coat and tie.
Q. Why are you dressed up?

A. It's Sunday.

Q. Describe the area, the countryside around you.

A. We're standing looking down at the river . . . it's a very small river, more like a creek; it runs into the sea right over there. There is a small walking bridge across it, and the stairs to the left go down to the water.

Q. What time of year is it?

A. Summer . . . everything is so green. Huge trees.

Q. What are you doing now?

A. I'm starting to climb down the stairs . . . oh . . . oh, no . . .

(Subject cries out in anguish and then stops talking.)

Maneuvering in time and asking additional questions uncovered the following facts: A long set of old wooden stairs led from the grassy picnic area to the rocky creek bed below—a drop of fifty or sixty feet. Samuel had started to climb down, with Margaret close behind him. His weight was too much for the aged structure; it collapsed, causing him to fall to his death on the rocks below. His wife had grabbed a portion of the stairs which remained anchored to the top, and she was thus saved.

Q. We are now going to move back in time, we are going to return to the time of your first meeting with Margaret. (Instructions given.)

A. We grew up together.

Q. Can you explain that a little more?

A. In the same town, we went to school together.

Q. All right, let's move in time once again, to the time that you and Margaret were married. (Instructions given.)

A. Many people are here . . . they are all congratulating us.

Q. Where were you married?

A. In the church.

Q. Where are you right now?

A. At Johnathan's house . . . party.

Q. How old are you and Margaret?

A. I'm twenty-four, she's twenty-three.

Q. Where will you live now?

A. On the plantation.

Q. Your plantation?

A. Yes.

Q. You must be wealthy if you own a plantation.

A. I inherited it from my parents when they died.

Q. Do you have a lot of money?

A. A little, not a lot.

Q. What kind of crops do you grow?

A. Cotton . . . some tobacco.

Q. Do you have slaves?

A. Yes.

Q. What do you feel toward your slaves?

A. They're good workers . . . I have their respect.

Q. Do you ever have any trouble with them?

A. Very seldom . . . usually fights among themselves.

Q. Where is your plantation located?

A. Several miles east of town on the coastal road.

Q. Are you close to the coast?

A. If it weren't for all the trees, you could see the sea from our front porch . . . across the road.

Q. What is the closest large town?

A. Biloxi is a day away.

Q. What year is it?

A. 1810.

Q. All right, let's move forward in time a little way until you and Margaret leave the party. (Instructions given.)

A. We're in the surrey . . . going home.

Q. Are you happy?

A. Yes, I certainly am.

Q. Move forward in time to when you arrive home, and describe the situation as you arrive, as it unfolds. (Instructions given.)

A. The house is there to the left . . . we're going up the drive and I stopped under the carriage entrance. Johna came out . . . he's holding the horses . . . he's smiling and talking to us. We're going into the house.

Q. I want you to describe the house to me as you go in.
A. These stairs lead up to the front entry. The main room is there to the right. That was my mother's piano. These stairs lead upstairs to the bedrooms and the second-story veranda.

Q. Is your plantation one of the largest in the area?
A. One of the smallest.

Q. How many rooms?
A. Three bedrooms upstairs and the veranda. Downstairs there is the main room, the side porch, Jennie's room and the kitchen.

Q. Who is Jennie?
A. She does the housework and cooking.

Q. Do you have any other house servants?
A. "No . . . old Johna helps out sometimes . . . and he takes care of the horses.

Q. What is your house made of?
A. Wood.

Q. What color is it?
A. White.

Q. Are there any brick houses in your area?
A. Many in Biloxi.

Q. Can you describe your wife, Margaret, to me?
A. She's beautiful . . . her hair is long and dark.

Q. How tall is she?
A. Five feet four inches.

Q. Have you planned to marry for a long time?
A. Yes . . . but my parents died on the boat, we had to wait.

Q. What happened?
A. An accident in the bay.

Q. Do you have any problems in your life at this time?
A. No.

Q. What will Margaret do now?
A. What do you mean?

Q. What will her duties be?
A. She'll have no duties.

Q. What will she do with her time?
A. She loves horses, she'll ride a lot, she'd like to start breeding them . . . she'll sew . . . see her friends.

Q. All right, let's move forward in time a little, move forward to a situation of importance that develops. (Instructions given.)

A. I'm in town standing in the street. Several men are coming this way and . . . and I'm joining them. We're all walking into the tobacco barn.

Q. What is a tobacco barn?

A. Where the leaves are stored . . . hung to dry.

Q. Is it like a regular barn?

A. No . . . no, it has individual rooms. We all bring our crops here. One of the men is mad . . . we're checking the rooms.

Q. What is he mad about?

A. It's all right now.

Q. What is all right now?

A. He thought they were stealing, but it was a mistake.

Q. Let's return to Margaret now, the next time you see her. (Instructions given.)

A. We're climbing into the surrey.

Q. Where are you?

A. Still in town. Margaret has been shopping.

Q. What did she buy?

A. Yardage and some things at the store . . . a friend was helping her finish a couple of dresses.

Q. Let's move forward to the time you get back home. What is happening now?

A. She's trying on the dresses . . . to show me.

Q. Do you like them?

A. Yes.

Q. What do you feel about your relationship with your wife now?

A. What do you mean?

Q. What do you feel, do you really love her, do you have a good sexual relationship? It is all right to tell me, you feel easy in telling me.

A. Yes . . . we get along very well. We spend a great deal of time in bed.

Q. Sleeping?

A. No . . . no . . . loving.

Q. Does Margaret like to make love as much as you do?

A. She certainly does.

Q. All right, let's now move forward to the last day of your life. You will not have died, you will not have crossed over into spirit, but it will be the last day of your life as Samuel. (Instructions given.)

A. Margaret and I are going for a ride.

Q. Horseback?

A. No, in the surrey.

Q. Where are you going?

A. To the picnic place above the river.

Q. Let's move forward to the time you get there. What are you doing now?

A. We're just strolling around.

Q. Are there any other people there?

A. Over on the other side.

Q. Do you know them?

A. Sure.

Q. All right, we are going to move forward in time. You will already have gone through the death experience, crossing over into spirit without pain and without emotion. (Instructions given.) Tell me what you are experiencing now.

A. Margaret is crying . . . oh, she's crying . . . they're helping her and she's crying. . . . I can't do anything, I'm floating . . . I seem to be floating.

Q. What is happening now?

A. They're climbing down to the rocks . . . John and his boy. . . . Somebody is lying down there.

Q. Isn't that you? Didn't the stairs collapse and you fell down?

A. I don't know. I think so.

Q. What is happening now?

A. They say he is dead. . . . Margaret is crying . . . she fainted, I think.

Q. Tell me how you feel now.

A. Fine. . . . I just keep floating . . . I don't know.

Q. Where is Margaret now?

A. They're taking her into town.

Q. Let's move forward in time a little way. What are you doing now?

A. The doctor gave her something to go to sleep.

Q. Is there anyone else there with you now?

A. My father . . . but . . . he's dead.

The subject was given the posthypnotic suggestion to remember everything he had seen and experienced, then told to awaken relaxed and refreshed.

"How do you feel?" I asked.

"That was really an experience. It was her. I know it was her. She didn't look like she does now, but I know it was her. The thing that bothers me, though, is that we didn't get to spend much time together in that life, either."

"There may be a karmic reason for that. We could go further back in another session if you'd like," I told him. "Are there any obvious tie-ins between that life and your present one?"

"Not on my part, but the part about the horses . . . Sharon loves them. She trains jumpers, and at least a few years ago she was living for the day she could get a horse of her own.

"Is there any way I could find out more, or verify any of what I just saw?' he asked.

"Well, I didn't go after a great deal of facts that might be on record. To the best of my knowledge, record keeping was not a big thing in the early 1800s, but you could certainly check out Biloxi . . . when it was founded, brick buildings, the kind of crops grown in that area at that time, things like that. We could always take you back under just to search for exact names and places, although sometimes this sort of information is harder to obtain. Today I was more interested in your prior relationship. If you'd like I can put you in touch with a psychic friend of mine. You can go to her for a reading. I'd suggest you take along three photographs . . . say one of your first wife, one of Sharon, and one of your present wife. Give them to her and see what she can tell you."

David called a few days later to tell me that he had been able to verify the facts we had uncovered about that particular area of Mississippi in 1810. He also said that he had gone to the psychic and that when he gave her the photographs she put her hands upon them and concentrated for several minutes. She then picked up the photo of Sharon and told him that she was a very old soul, much older than the other two. She saw David and her together in another time and told him that Sharon was a little shorter and her hair wasn't as long in that life. She saw them married, but told him that they were tragically separated shortly after their marriage. "You have strong soul ties with this woman," was the psychic's summation of her discussion about David and Sharon's relationship.

David

Second Regression Session

May 1975

As part of the research for this book, I called David and asked him if he would be interested in doing another session, in which we would attempt to find an earlier lifetime tie with Sharon, if in fact one did exist. Although they had shared only a small moment in time in this life and the last one, the intensity of their relationship interested me. David instantly agreed, and the following regression took place a couple of days later:

Hypnosis induced and regression preparation completed. The subject was then given the following instructions: "I want you to move backward in time, way backward in time to the lifetime in which you and the woman you know as Sharon were first together. Move to an event of importance that took place in that lifetime, if indeed you have known such a prior existence." (Instructions given.)

Q. What do you see and what are you doing?

A. I'm on a ship.

Q. Are you at sea?

A. Yes.

Q. Are there others there with you?

A. Yes, many.

Q. What do you do—are you a seaman or a passenger?

A. I'm a soldier.

Q. Is this a military ship, and if so, what are your duties?

A. We're transporting three important men to Egypt.

Q. Where are you coming from? I want you to tell me the name or spell it out.

A. I can see it . . . Colardan." (Phonetic spelling.)

Q. Was your assignment to pick up these men?

A. Yes, they are very important.

Q. What do they look like?

A. Two of them are older . . . have white hair . . . one of them is not older.

Q. Are they officials?

A. They are from the other land, they are important . . . I don't know why.

Q. How are they dressed?

A. White . . . gold-colored trim . . . like a skirt . . . high laced sandals.

Q. Let's move forward in time to the time you actually return from Egypt. (Instructions given.)

At this point the subject describes entering the Egyptian port. "It's like a long rectangle of water; there are two other large ships and many small boats; the buildings are on the hill above the harbor. They are earth-colored, and the large one has a dome on the top." He then escorted his official visitors to a nearby city.

Q. How old are you at this time?

A. Twenty-nine.

Q. I want to know your name.

A. Krean. (Phonetic spelling.)

Q. Who are you in service to? Who is the leader of Egypt now?

A. The Altan is Reienta. (Phonetic spelling.)

(Note: This answer seems confusing, but as the regression proceeds, it becomes obvious that Krean is living in Atlantean times, well before the development of Egypt as we historically know it. Atlantis was thought to exist in the Atlantic Ocean between 50,000 and 10,000 B.C.)

Q. All right, let's move forward to time when you meet someone who is important to you. (Instructions given.)

A. I am within one of the temple buildings . . . beautiful . . . beautiful.

Q. What are you doing there?

A. I am to deliver these papers to the priests.

(Note: In discussing the regression later, David recalled that the papers were in a long roll and sealed around the middle with a metallic band that carried a wax-type seal with a symbol impressed on it.)

Q. Do you know what these papers contain?

A. No.

Q. What are you doing right now?

A. Someone else has taken the papers.

Q. Was it the priest?

A. No, someone else . . . I'm standing looking at a girl.

Q. Do you know who she is?

A. She is in training here.

Q. What is she doing now?

A. She's smiling at me. . . . I walked over to her. . . . I can't be here.

Q. Why not?

A. I was to deliver the papers and leave. No one is allowed here.

Q. Why not?

A. I was to deliver the papers and leave. No one is allowed here.

Q. What are you doing now?

A. I'm talking to her.

Q. What is she saying?

A. We're just talking . . . she's . . . she's not supposed to be talking to me either.

Q. Can you describe to me what she looks like?

A. She's beautiful . . . long dark hair . . . she has on a white . . . uh . . . it's long . . . it comes down from the middle of the back of her hair . . . it hides a lot of her hair . . . but it's real thin, you can see through it. She has something around her neck.

Q. Is it a symbol or just an ornament?

A. It's a symbol of this order.

Q. Let's move forward a few minutes until you leave or until something happens. (Instructions given.)

A. He's telling me to leave . . . he's very mad.

Q. Is he a guard?

A. He has a bald head . . . he has on robes, and he's telling me to leave. . . . I'll be in trouble.

Q. "Let's move to a time that you see her again, if in until something happens. (Instructions given.)

A. I'm with her.

Q. Where are you at?

A. Just a short way from the temple.

Q. Did you plan to meet her or did you just happen to meet her?

A. Planned to meet her.

Q. Did you send her word or did you go into the temple again?

A. No, I didn't go in there again. (Subject shows disbelief that such a question even be asked . . . also fear.)

Q. What are you saying to her at this time?

A. I have my arms around her . . . we're just talking. . . . She . . . she's been there for many, many years.

Q. Was she raised there from a child?

A. I don't know.

Q. Is she happy within the temple environment?

A. I don't think so . . . the priests often misuse the women, although they would absolutely deny it. . . . They are not what they appear to be sometimes.

Q. Do you mean sexually?

A. Yes . . . and other ways.

Q. What is she in training for?

A. The priests train many young women . . . they'll work within the order.

Q. Are the priests very powerful in your community?

A. Oh, yes! (Very emphatic.)

Q. Will she have much time with you now, or will she have to go back into the temple?

A. Oh . . . she'll have to go back . . . if they discover she's gone. . . ."

Q. She shouldn't be there then—is that correct?

A. Oh, no.

Q. Are you planning to meet with her again?

A. I want to.

Q. Let's move forward in time until an important event transpires. (Instructions given.)

A. I'm in trouble.

Q. Who are you in trouble with?

A. Everybody.

Q. Because you talked with her?

A. Yes. (In discussing the regression later, Daxid explained that he knew he was in trouble for talking with her in the temple. That if they had known he had met her outside, he would have been killed.)

Q. What is happening now?

A. They're yelling.

Q. Where are you?

A. Room . . . one of the main official buildings. . . . There is a desk . . . not separate, it's part of the wall . . . goes out . . . I'm in trouble.

Q. What type of disciplinary measures will they take?

A. I'll be reduced in rank.

Q. What rank are you now?

A. Fourth Level.

Q. So they'll reduce you in rank. . . . Are there any further measures they will take?

A. If I see her again, they will.

Q. How long has it been since you talked to her?

A. Yesterday.

Q. I want you now to tell me her name.

A. L-a-r-a-n-a . . . Larana.

Q. Let's move forward in time again until something more important happens. (Instructions given.)

A. We're in a boat.

Q. Who else is with you?

A. She is . . . Larana.

Q. Is it a large boat?

A. No.

Q. Where are you going?

A. We're leaving.

Q. Escaping?

A. Yes.

Q. Is there anyone following you at this time? Do they know you have left?

A. Probably half of Egypt.

Q. Is Larana a very important person in your society?

A. No . . . it's . . . it's not that. . . . It can't be done . . . everyone will be in trouble now.

Q. So everyone will be angered by the fact that you have taken her away?

A. I suppose.

Q. Do you have a destination?

A. A place I was once . . . a couple of years ago.

Q. When you were in the military?

A. A different land.

Q. Did Larana go with you of her own free will?

A. Oh, yes.

Q. Let's move forward in time until you reach your destination, or some other important event takes place. (Instructions given.)

A. I don't know where we are . . . there're trees . . . but this isn't . . . this isn't where I was before.

Q. Then no one has caught up with you?

A. No.

Q. How much time has elapsed since you left Egypt?

A. Oh, several days . . . maybe ten.

Q. What are you doing now?

A. We're just walking now . . . I don't know where we are.

Q. Are there any cities nearby?

A. I don't know . . . just walking . . . trying to stay along the coast so we don't get lost. . . . We might get lost in there . . . hopelessly . . . lost. . . . We'll stay along the coast.

Q. What are your plans at this time?

A. To find a place where we can live.

Q. How old are you now?

A. Thirty.

Q. We're going to move forward now until something very important happens. (Instructions given.)

A. In our home . . . she's . . . Larana's had a baby . . . she's fine.

Q. Is it a boy or a girl?

A. A boy.

Q. If you are in your home, there must be a town nearby.

A. Yes . . . we live in the town.

Q. What is the name of the town?

A. Melean. (Phonetic spelling.)

Q. Are you still on the African continent?

A. I don't know that . . . we crossed south . . . crossed the sea at the shortest point.

Q. Was it a very large sea?

A. Well, if you go west, it opens into the ocean.

(Note: According to modern-day geography this doesn't track, but possibly during this time Egypt extended up into what would now be Syria. If this is so, they could have crossed the Mediterranean, south at its shortest point, then worked their way along the coast to what is now Libya. Traveling west through the Mediterranean would have taken them to the Atlantic Ocean.)

Q. What are the townspeople's feelings toward you at this time? Do they regard you as an outsider?

A. No . . . no, we get along very well.

Q. Have the Egyptians given up their search for you?

A. I don't know . . . never heard.

Q. You do not live in fear then?

A. No . . . Larana fears for her family. . . . Many people may have been punished . . . for what she . . . for what we did . . . but there is no way to know.

Q. Are you happy at this time?

A. Oh, yes.

Q. What do you do to make a living? What do you do with your time?

A. I'm working with wood.

Q. Do you build things then?

A. I'm working on the spokes to a wheel.

Q. What else do you do?

A. We fish.

Q. Do you sell or trade these fish?

A. No, they're just for my family.

Q. How old are you now?

A. Thirty-two.

Q. Let's move forward in time until something very important happens. (Instructions given.)

A. Many, many ships . . . many . . . way below. . . . We're very high above them . . . the sea is full of ships.

Q. Are these ships from another land?

A. They're sure not from here.

Q. Do they look like Egyptian ships? Do you recognize them?

A. No, I don't.

Q. Are they threatening, or are they friendly?

A. None of us know . . . the sea is full of ships.

Q. Who is there with you?

A. The people of Melean.

Q. Let's move forward in time until you find out why the ships are there. (Instructions given.)

A. That's a bad place to moor a ship . . . they'll wish they hadn't landed there . . . when the tide goes out.

Q. Have they all landed?

A. No, only one.

Q. Tell me about what is happening.

A. We're talking to them . . . they're from the other land out in the sea.

Q. What do you know of this land out in the sea?

A. I have been there twice . . . to escort important men to Egypt.

Q. What is the name of the land?

A. Atlantis.

Q. Before you told me you had picked up the men in Colardan—can you explain that?

A. Colardan is an Atlantean port city.

Q. You are now talking or listening to the conversations

with the men from the ships. Tell me what is being said.

A. They are way too far south . . . way too far . . . they had . . . storms drove them south . . . now they're short of supplies.

Q. Are they friendly to you?

A. Oh, yes.

Q. What do their ships look like?

A. Well . . . they . . . they are narrow . . . they have a very . . . striped square sail which is not needed but is used when they're coming in. . . . They put out the square sails . . . they are very colorful . . . but not necessary.

Q. How are they driven or powered?

A. I don't understand how the power works . . . it works . . . it's below the deck. I've seen it, but I don't understand it.

Q. What else are they talking to you about?

A. We've told them the shortest route to their destination, but we can't supply them . . . we're a very small . . . we can't supply them at all.

Q. Why are there so many ships? Have they explained that to you?

A. They are traveling to Egypt . . . they're only here because of the storm.

Q. Are they warships?

A. Oh, no.

Q. So they have friendly relations with Egypt, is that correct?

A. Yes, of course.

Q. I want you to tell me what year this is.

A. I don't understand . . . the season . . . of . . . the twenty-eighth period . . . the summer season to the twenty-eighth period.

Q. Is this the Egyptian way to relate time?

A. Everyone calls it the . . . it is the twenty-eighth period.

Q. Let's move forward again to the next important event that takes place in your life as Krean. (Instructions given.)

A. Another child is born . . . a girl.

Q. How old is your son at this time?

A. Seven.

Q. Are you and Larana happy now?

A. Yes, we're very happy . . . life is so simple here.

Q. What do you and Larana do together?

A. We sail . . . we help each other with the things that are to be done. . . . While I'm fishing she makes our clothing and takes care of the children. . . . Sometimes I draw.

Q. Then you're glad you left Egypt.

A. Very much.

Q. Let's move forward in time again, way forward until the next very important event takes place in your life. (Instructions given.)

A. In the boat . . . the sea is really . . . tossing. . . . I hurt my arm, my arm hurts so bad. (Subject shows the pain.)

Q. How did you hurt your arm?

A. Tossed down in the boat . . . I think it's broken.

Q. Are there any others there with you?

A. Two others.

Q. What is happening now? Are you trying to get to shore?

A. Oh, yes . . . we're going over . . . capsizing . . . (Subject begins very heavy breathing, then calms by himself.)

Q. Are you swimming?

A. (No reaction from subject.)

When maneuvered in time, further questioning showed that Krean had drowned. He was an older man at this time.

(End of second session)

"I've never liked being out on the ocean in boats," David said. "You've never seen anyone do as much sidestepping as I do every time a chance comes up. My wife and I go to Mexico a lot, upper Baja. People are always asking us to go out fishing with them, and thus far

I've avoided it. The few times I have been in small boats, I've always felt uneasy."

"This could be the reason, or at least part of it if you've never had a bad boating experience in this life," I said.

We talked about the regression for a while. Although I've regressed many people into the Atlantean time periods, and generally know what to expect, many of the situations encountered here were new to me.

"Do you suppose that's it, or do you think Sharon and I have been together in still other lifetimes?" he asked.

"Personally I'd bet money on it. Let's say theoretically that you were living in the mid-Atlantean period of about 30,000 B.C. You could have lived literally hundreds of lives since then. From my experience, the chance that Sharon would have been a part of all of them would be very rare. But I'm sure she was known to you in many lifetimes."

David smiled. "I don't think I have time to find out about hundreds of lifetimes. I'd use up all the time I have left in this one."

Kathy and John

KATHY AND JOHN ARE ONE OF OUR CLOSEST NEIGHBORS, and shortly after our arrival in the mountain community of Groom Creek, Arizona, they became close friends. Our common professions alone would have created a bond, but their warmth and openness assure it. John is a writer/photographer, working as a stringer for the *Phoenix Republic* newspaper, and as a free-lancer on any other writing assignments he can find. In addition, the couple teaches yoga at an outdoor survival-oriented college in Prescott. Both are accomplished astrologers and longtime vegetarians. Their lives are an active and happy routine of physical and spiritual harmony.

Kathy is now twenty-one and John is twenty-eight; they have been married a year and a half and have no children. Monetary needs are very small, amounting to only a few hundred dollars a month. Which is all they usually make.

During the winter Kathy asked if I would consider doing a group regression for her yoga class. Part of her teaching includes metaphysical philosophy, and thus reincarnation. We decided to stage the regression in their cabin opposed to the school, so eighteen students gathered around the old wood stove and in the cabin loft. Yogis are trained in deep breathing and relaxation, so as a general rule they make exceptionally good hypnosis subjects.

Of the eighteen students and two instructors present

that afternoon, all but one experienced vivid past-life impressions. Most of the students were too young for the sort of relationship ties I was seeking as research for this book, but Kathy was a fine subject.

In the ensuing months I taught her self-hypnosis and made her a self-induction tape, structured to eliminate a monthly problem of extreme menstrual cramps and abdominal pain. By the second month of working with the technique, she experienced no menstrual discomfort, for the first time in her adult life. She was also a perfectly conditioned hypnosis subject by this time.

We had often talked about exploring a past-life tie between Kathy and John. Their astrology charts gave evidence of prior lives together, and their present life was another strong indication. But living in the mountains is very conducive to procrastination. A spare afternoon for experimental regressions is much more likely to result in several families, kids, dogs, and adults, crowding into a couple of pickup trucks and gravitating to the swimming hole on a nearby creek for an afternoon of skinny dipping.

Finally on a rainy Sunday afternoon in June we decided to take the time to explore the past.

Kathy

First Regression Session

July 1975

Hypnosis induced and regression preparation completed. The following instructions were then given:

"If you have known your husband John in a former incarnation, in another life, in another time, we are now going to travel backward in time to the time of an early meeting that took place between you in the last lifetime you were together. If you have not known him before, on

the count of eleven you will speak up and tell me so."
(Instructions given.)

Q. What do you see and what are you doing?
A. I'm sitting on a hill; there's grass.
Q. Can you tell me any more about the situation?
A. There is a man . . . pine trees behind us . . . mountains across.
Q. What is the man doing at this time?
A. Talking.
Q. How do you feel toward this man?
A. We're good friends.
Q. Can you tell me how you are dressed?
A. Long green dress.
Q. What is it made of? Is it fancy, or is it a basic dress?
A. It's cotton with flowers. . . .
Q. What is the man wearing?
A. A short coat, long pants, with boots . . . a hat.
Q. Can you tell me what you are talking about?
A. Just about me and the mountains.
Q. Where do you live? Is the place you're sitting near your home?
A. Yes . . . in a valley.
Q. Who do you live with?
A. My mother and father.
Q. How long will it take you to walk to your home in the valley?
A. Probably about forty-five minutes.
Q. What about your friend—does he also live nearby?
A. No.
Q. Where does he live?
A. Far away.
Q. Has he come here for the specific purpose of visiting you?
A. I am not sure.
Q. Is he about your age?
A. A few years older.
Q. Can you tell me if you have any brothers and sisters?
A. One brother and one sister.
Q. Are they older or younger than you?

A. Younger.

Q. Let's move forward in time to the time you will be arriving back home. (Instructions given.) What are you doing?

A. Eating dinner.

Q. Is your friend there with you, the one on the hill?

A. Yes.

Q. Who fixed the dinner?

A. My mother, sister, and myself.

Q. What are you having for dinner?

A. Ham.

Q. What else besides the ham?

A. Potatoes and corn.

Q. All right, was the ham purchased at the store, or was this something your family raised?

A. Raised.

Q. Then you do have a farm?

A. Yes.

Q. You have livestock—is this correct?

A. Yes.

Q. What other livestock do you have?

A. Sheep, horses, and chickens.

Q. How old are you at this time?

A. Twenty.

Q. Is the young man with you on the hill . . . is he a boy-friend or fiancé? Tell me about your relationship.

A. He wants me to go away with him.

Q. By going with him does that mean you would be marrying him?

A. Yes.

Q. How long have you known him?

A. A couple of weeks.

Q. What is his name?

A. Emil.

Q. What is your name?

A. Gretchen.

Q. Can you tell me the country you live in?

A. Germany.

Q. Was the clothing you described on the young man a uniform, or regular clothes?

A. Just clothes . . . for hiking.

Q. Let's move forward in time, to when you make a decision to leave with the man or decide to stay. (Instructions given.)

A. My father says I have to go.

Q. So he has made the decision for you? What do you feel about this decision?

A. I like him. But I am not sure.

Q. Let's move forward in time a full year. (Instructions given.) Tell me what you see.

A. A tower . . . in the city.

Q. Is Emil there with you at this time?

A. Yes.

Q. Did you get married?

A. Yes.

Q. What are you doing?

A. In the park sitting down.

Q. Do you live in the city?

A. Yes, he is rich.

Q. He has a lot of money?

A. Yes.

Q. What does he do with his time?

A. He's a businessman.

Q. Can you tell me anything about the business?

A. It's dry goods.

Q. You're now twenty-some years of age, living in Germany. Can you tell me the year?

A. 1919.

Q. Tell me about your life now. Are you happy with your life? Do you like living in the city?

A. I miss the country.

Q. Do you ever get a chance to visit your parents?

A. Sometimes.

Q. So they live very far away then?

A. Pretty far.

Q. When you do go back to see them, how do you travel?

A. Buggy.

Q. Does someone drive you, or do you take yourself?

A. We have a driver.

Q. So he is really quite wealthy, if you do have your own driver.

A. Oh, yes.

Q. Are you planning to have any children?

A. I am three months pregnant.

Q. At this time?

A. Yes.

Q. Are you happy about this?

A. Yes.

Q. What is the political situation in Germany at this time? Is there unrest or is there peace?

A. . . . Oh . . . two thoughts.

Q. Two thoughts . . . can you explain this?

A. Some think the government will fall quickly. . . .

Q. What is the other train of thought?

A. The rich will win.

Q. What is yours and your husband's feelings? . . . What would you like to see happen? . . . What does he talk about?

A. He doesn't talk about the business with me . . . I don't know very much about it . . . he's very quiet.

Q. We're going to move forward in time about six months . . . to the time the baby is born. (Instructions given.)

A. Having pains . . . in a room.

Q. Where are you at this time?

A. In my room.

Q. Are you in your room or is this a hospital room?

A. My room.

Q. Let's move forward in time to right after the birth. (Instructions given.)

A. I am very tired. I had twins.

Q. What sex?

A. Girls.

Q. Who else is there at this time?

A. Emil . . . and the nurse.

Q. Was there a doctor who delivered the babies?

A. No . . . they came too soon.

Q. Are the babies all right?

A. Yes.

Q. What do you feel about having twins? Was this a surprise?

A. I was so big . . . it had to be twins . . . it was expected.

Q. Do you feel good about this?

A. I don't know, it's a lot of work.

Q. You're going to feel easy . . . you will no longer feel tired. Tell me what your husband is doing.

A. He owns two dry-goods stores.

Q. Is the business good?

A. Yes . . . but there's been trouble with poor people.

Q. What are the poor people doing?

A. Windows smashed.

Q. Why would they do something like that?

A. They can't pay.

Q. Is there civil strife in Germany right now? . . . Can you describe the situation to me?

A. It's getting worse . . . I don't think we'll stay.

Q. What is the government doing about it at this time?

A. Nothing.

Q. All right, we're going to move forward in time . . . until an important event takes place. (Instructions given.)

A. I think . . . we're going to move back to the country.

Q. Why have you made the decision to move back to the country?

A. It's too dangerous for the children and me.

Q. There's much civil unrest . . . I take it?

A. Just against the very rich.

Q. So will Emil move back to the country with you?

A. Yes.

Q. What about his stores?

A. There are people who will run them.

Q. Will you go back to the area your parents live in?

A. Yes.

Q. How soon is this going to happen?

A. A couple of months.

Q. How old are your children at this time?

A. Five.

Q. Are they both healthy and doing fine?

A. Yes.

Q. Can you tell me the name of the city you live in at this time?

A. Heidelberg.

Q. We're going to move forward in time to the time you leave to return to the country. (Instructions given.)

A. . . . going down a dirt road.

Q. Are you in a buggy?

A. Yes, there are flowers, grass, trees.

Q. How do you feel about the fact that you are leaving?

A. I'm glad.

Q. What does Emil feel?

A. He's disturbed.

Q. Is he worried about his business back in Heidelberg?

A. Yes.

Q. Let's move forward until another important event takes place in your life. (Instructions given.)

A. The house is built . . . built a new house.

Q. Is this close to your parents' home?

A. A few miles.

Q. Who built the house . . . did you hire someone to come build the house?

A. My father helped . . . Emil.

Q. Is it very big?

A. Yes.

Q. What is the situation now? Do you get much news about the situation in Germany?

A. Looking . . . waiting for something big.

Q. O.K. . . . let's move forward until that time, until something big does happen and you hear about it. (Instructions given.)

A. The stores were both on fire . . . more riots. We have nothing left in the city.

Q. Have you lost everything?

A. Almost everything.

(Note: Historically the 1920s in Germany was a time of runaway inflation such as the world had never known. The mark literally became worthless. Within a few years it took 4.2 trillion marks to buy what one mark had previously purchased. The natural result was civil strife and upheaval.)

Q. Let's move ahead in time at least ten years. (Instructions given.)

A. Some time in the thirties.

Q. How old are your children now?

A. They . . . are young women.

Q. Has Germany been at war?

A. Not yet.

Q. Let's move forward in time . . . until Germany goes to war . . . you will be able to tell me what effect it has on you. (Instructions given.)

A. A messenger says they're marching . . . and we're scared . . . because we're not protected.

Q. What does your husband feel?

A. He's scared.

Q. Will he have to join the army?

A. Yes.

Q. Let's move forward to the time your husband has to go to war . . . to the time of your parting. (Instructions given.)

A. He's going with my father.

Q. Your father is also going to war?

A. Yes.

Q. Are they volunteering?

A. My father is . . . my brother is gone.

Q. What is your feeling at this time?

A. Very scared . . . no men. . . .

Q. What about your mother?

A. She has to move into our house.

Q. Then you will be living with your mother and your daughters?

A. Yes.

Q. Let's move forward in time to an important event that takes place in your life, Gretchen. (Instructions given.)

A. There are soldiers on our land.

Q. Are they German soldiers?

A. Yes.

Q. What is the situation . . . how do you feel toward them?

A. I hate them. (Subject shows anger and frustration.)

Q. How are they acting toward you?

A. They are ruining our land. . . . (Subject shows strong emotion and is given calming suggestions.)

Q. What have they done to ruin the land?

A. They have taken all the food out . . . the crops. . . .

Q. All the crops that you have planted?

A. Yes.

Q. Are they willing to pay you for them to compensate you in any way?

A. No.

Q. How do they act toward you?

A. No respect.

Q. But they have not harmed you in any way? . . . Other than taking your crops?

A. No.

Q. Let's move forward to the next important event that transpires. (Instructions given.)

A. My husband died.

Q. How did you receive word of this?

A. Soldiers.

Q. They came and told you?

A. They never left.

Q. How was Emil killed—do you know?

A. Fighting.

Q. Was he fighting on German land or elsewhere?

A. On the border.

Q. What news do you have of your father and your brother?

A. None.

Q. How long ago did you learn that your husband was killed?

A. Two weeks ago.

Q. Are you all right now?

A. No . . . it's hard . . . the soldiers came and tried to come into the house.

Q. Have you been able, thus far, to stop them . . . to deter them from coming into the house?

A. Yes.

Q. Have you had any contact with their commander?

A. Yes . . . but he just orders me for Germany.

Q. He feels you should cooperate in anything as a loyal German?

A. Yes.

Q. Have your daughters been bothered by the soldiers?

A. Yes. . . . (Very emotional.)

Q. Can you tell me about it?

A. Oh . . . no . . . one got her and raped her.

Q. Was anything done to punish the soldier?

A. No. (Much disgust in subject's voice.)

Q. So I take it you are living in a situation of fear at this time?

A. Yes.

Q. (Instructions given to rise above the emotional pain of the situation.) Now let's move forward in time to the next important situation. (Instructions given.)

A. Running away.

Q. Whom are you running from?

A. Almost everyone . . . the soldiers.

Q. You have left your home then, I take it.

A. Yes.

Q. How long ago did you leave your home?

A. A month ago.

Q. Do you have a destination . . . or are you just trying to get away?

A. We're trying to get to Sweden.

Q. Did you have more trouble with the soldiers?

A. Yes.

Q. What else did they do besides raping your daughter?

A. They scared my mother . . . she had a heart attack. . . . (Voice cracking.)

Q. Did she die?

A. Yes.

Q. What about yourself—were you actually molested by them?

A. Yes.

Q. What about your other daughter?

A. No.

Q. So you felt you had to run, and this was the only thing to do?

A. Yes.

Q. Let's move forward in time until something important happens. (Instructions given.)

A. We're being put on a train . . . there's so many people. (Subject starts to cry and is given calming suggestions.)

Q. Where are they taking you to?

A. To a camp.

Q. Why should you as a German be put in a camp?

A. They're crazy. (Tears are now running down the subject's cheeks.)

Q. Are your daughters with you at this time?

A. Oh . . . no . . . only one. . . .

Q. What happened to the other one?

A. She got separated at the train.

Q. You don't know where she is?

A. No.

Q. We're going to move forward in time. . . . (Before the instructions were completed the subject screamed, grabbed her stomach, and was crying uncontrollably.)

A. My stomach . . . (Extremely frightened.)

Q. What's happening?

A. They're ripping it apart.

(Because of subject's extreme reaction she was immediately removed from the situation and returned to the present. Several minutes were spent in giving calming, peaceful suggestions and a posthypnotic command that she forget everything she had just seen and experienced.)

(End of first session)

Often, if a regression proves to be extremely traumatic, I will block the experience from the subject's mind. Then later we can discuss the situation and usually listen to the tape together. Although the subject is listening to his own experience, it is much easier in this way to detach emotionally.

The regression had been performed with Kathy lying on the bed in our bedroom. When she awakened, it was obvious that the suggestion to forget what she had experienced had only partially taken. The emotional trauma had simply been too much to block out entirely. Her trance had been so deep that she remained lying down, rubbing her hands to bring back the circulation. She was remembering enough to know it had been a heavy experience.

There had been others present throughout the regression. We all discussed the situation and went over the tape. Kathy identified her pain as Gretchen with her own present-day menstrual problems.

"Since physical problems can often be a carry-over from another lifetime, I wonder if my monthly pains have been related to what happened in that prison camp in Germany?" she asked.

(Note: Judging from my own experiences with regressions, and those of colleagues, this is all the more likely to happen when an entity is reborn quickly. Kathy had obviously spent very few years on the other side before reincarnating.)

Several days later we held a second session. I did not want to return her to the scene of the prison camp, so it was decided to examine the past life from the perspective of "Spirit."

Second Regression Session

June 1975

Hypnosis induced and regression preparation complete. The following instructions were then given:

"You are now going to return to the lifetime of Gretchen in Germany, but it will be immediately after you have experienced death . . . you will already have crossed over into spirit, feeling no physical pain, but from this perspective you will be able to answer all of my questions about your life as Gretchen. On the count of eleven you will find yourself in spirit, immediately after leaving your earthly body." (Instructions given.)

Q. Tell me what you are experiencing at this time.
A. I'm floating . . . just floating.
Q. Can you see the body you just left?
A. Yes . . . below me.
Q. Tell me about the situation.
A. My body's on a table . . . it's got dark hair . . . my stomach is all torn apart.
Q. What did they hope to achieve in doing this, in operating on you?
A. There is no reason. (Subject shows disgust in her voice.)
Q. What was the purpose? There must have been some purpose.
A. To replace one of my organs with an animal organ.

At the end of this session the subject was instructed to remember everything about the experience. From a superconscious mind level she was instructed to absorb a full understanding of this lifetime, much like a high-speed tape recorder moving through an entire lifetime on fast rewind. Through this knowledge, which was discussed after the session, and through additional questions and answers under hypnosis, we achieved the following understanding. Gretchen had not been Jewish, but was picked up while trying to escape Germany, so was thought to be Jewish by her captors. Her dark complexion only helped to create the impression. She obviously felt much hostility toward the Nazis, which she freely expressed while in camp. Emil had not become a Nazi, to her knowledge, but limited correspondence did not assure that he had not joined the party. In their present lives John is Jewish, Kathy isn't. Both of Gretchen's daughters also died in the camp. Gretchen was close to fifty at the time of her death. When asked from the spirit level what had been the primary learning of the German lifetime, she answered, "My daughters taught me how to serve, they took much care.

Q. All right, we are going to let go of this and we are going to maneuver in time once again. If you have known John, who also was your husband Emil in Germany, I now want you to move backward in time to the very first earth lifetime in which you knew each other. It will be at the time of an important event which took place between you. If there have been no others, on the count of eleven you will speak up and tell me so. (Instructions given.)

When asked what she saw and what she was doing, Kathy explained that she was looking for a man. He would soon be leaving, and she wanted to say her goodbyes. Through additional questions we found that she was a citizen of Lemuria.

(Note: Lemuria, or Mu, is a continent thought to have existed in the Pacific prior to and during the time of Atlantis. Although recent scientific discoveries are substantiating the fact that such a land mass and civilization probably did exist, most of the knowledge available has come through psychic channels, such as the Edgar Cayce readings, direct writing, and psychic or medium contact with deceased entities. These sources indicate that the civilization was highly evolved and psychically developed.)

Q. What is the situation now?
A. I've mentally drawn him to . . . he's been able to find me.
Q. Is it necessary that he leave?
A. He chose to leave. It is very difficult to find volunteers . . . he has the necessary skills that will be extremely helpful on the journey.
Q. What skills?
A. He is highly telepathic . . . he can keep in contact with the center from vast distances.
Q. Where is he going?
A. The ships are leaving because the land is so crowded . . . they know where the new lands lie.
Q. Can you describe your relationship with this man?
A. It is a combination of being friends and lovers.
Q. I take it you are very sad to see him go?

A. Yes . . . but we won't be separated in spirit.

Q. What do you yourself do at this time?

A. I work with color.

Q. Can you elaborate upon this?

A. I'm working with different hues and values . . . of color and the responses of different people to color, and how to put a color environment together in harmony.

Q. Are you talking about an environment to live in?

A. Yes . . . and for health . . . to let their mental and ' emotional energies flow naturally and smoothly, so that they can direct themselves in a spiritual way.

At this point in the regression I instructed Kathy to move forward in time to another important lifetime in which she and her husband had been together, if one existed. I stressed "important," realizing, as is so often the case, that the time span between the past and present offered literally hundreds of possibilities.

Q. What do you see and what are you doing?

A. I am inside the temple . . . I'm talking to a man . . . we are both in the priest order . . . he is a priest . . . I am a priestess. We are both very upset about the way things are going within the orders.

Q. What has you upset?

A. Recently some of the higher priests have been demanding that the people bring in personal sacrifices, such as gems, clothing, food . . . any material objects. The priests take them and hoard them.

Q. Tell me the name of the country you are living in at this time.

A. Egypt.

Q. Is there any form of marriage between yourself and the priests?

A. No . . . priests can't marry.

Q. What is your relationship, then?

A. A warm friendship.

Q. All right, we are going to move forward in time now to the last day of your life. You will not have died,

you will not have crossed over into spirit, but it
will be the last day of your life. (Instructions given.)
A. We're in a sparsely wooded area . . . near the desert.
Q. Tell me of the highlights of your life.
A. We left the order. I could not ask people to do what
I know was not right. We've lived by ourselves for
many years.
Q. You and the priest?
A. Yes.
Q. Let's move forward in time a little way . . . on the
count of five you will have experienced death without
pain and without emotion, and you will be in spirit.
(Instructions given.) Now I want you to tell me how
you died.
A. An affliction of the lungs, but it was not extremely pain-
ful, for I had learned exercises in becoming a priestess
. . . how to alleviate pain.
Q. Was this in the "mystery schools"?
A. Yes.
(Note: Historically Egyptian mystery schools were meta-
physical training grounds for those in high places and the
priesthood.)
(End of second session)

The subject had been under hypnosis for a full hour;
I decided at this time to awaken her. Upon coming out
of the trance, Kathy explained that she had been told of
the Egyptian lifetime by a psychic in Virginia Beach,
Virginia, while she was teaching yoga there.

"He was a psychic harpist," she explained. "He's well
known and respected for his abilities in that part of the
country. Psychically he picks out your musical notes and
composes them in a lengthy composition, which I recorded
and have often used while meditating. The music matches
your vibrations and the result is very 'high.' While working with John and me, he picked up this Egyptian lifetime, explaining that the priests were getting lost in their
dogma and intellect and that we decided to leave . . . to
escape."

An obvious tie-in to the Lemurian incarnation is her

present love of art. Today she spends several hours a day, five days a week, training under a local artist who accepts small classes of students.

A few days later we did another regression. I was especially interested in Kathy and John's spiritual evolution.

I decided first to seek out a lifetime in which Kathy and John had been together, in which they had experienced their greatest growth.

Third Regression Session

July 1975

Hypnosis induced and regression preparation completed. The following instructions were then given: "We have previously examined three lifetimes in which you and John have been together. If there are more lifetimes in which you hav known each other, I now want you to return to the *most important* incarnation, from the standpoint of your own soul's growth . . . the lifetime in which you feel, through the knowledge in the memory banks of your subconscious mind, that you advanced yourself and your understanding further than in any other. If this life is one we have already examined, we will return, once again, to it." (Instructions given.)

Q. Tell me what you see, what you are experiencing at this time.
A. I'm near a beach . . . looking out . . . there's a large boat . . . big sails . . . they have crosses on them.
Q. Religious crosses?
A. It's . . . ah . . . Maltese cross.
Q. Is there anyone else there with you at this time?
A. Yes . . . but . . . but I don't have his form.

Q. What are you doing on the beach?
A. We wanted to go swimming . . . so we went to the beach.
Q. How far offshore is the boat?
A. About a half mile.
Q. What do you feel about the boat? Are you interested in it or fearful of it?
A. No . . . just curiosity.

Additional questions established that the boat carried no significance for the subject. She was experiencing a female incarnation, and the man she was with on the beach was her husband in her present life as Kathy. She was moved forward in time a little way.

Q. What are you doing now?
A. I'm walking through town.
Q. Can you describe the town?
A. The buildings have smooth surfaces . . . they're shiny . . . narrow walkway.
Q. Are there others present, and if so what are they doing?
A. People are selling at the market . . . walking around . . .
Q. Where are you going?
A. I'm going to meet a man . . . the one on the beach . . . we're talking about leaving together.
Q. Do you love this man?
A. Yes.
Q. Why would you both be leaving?
A. My parents don't like his parents.
Q. What can you tell me about the town you're in? It must be near the sea. Is it a fishing village?
A. Little fishing . . . mostly trading . . . compared to other towns, it is wealthy.
Q. What year is this?
A. I don't know that.
Q. Let's move forward in time until something important happens between you and this man. (Instructions given.)

A. We moved to Jerusalem, and we were married.

Q. All right, now we're going to move forward to a very important situation that takes place in the future. (Instructions given.)

A. I met Peter.

Q. Can you tell me about this experience?

A. He was preaching out near the square . . . and I waited to talk with him. . . . He came to our house for dinner . . . it was wonderful.

Q. Now you were not in Jerusalem at the time of the crucifixion—is that correct?

A. Yes, that is correct.

Q. Have you heard many people talk of this?

A. Yes . . . and I've seen others who have been crucified.

Q. Did Peter talk with you about the time he spent with Jesus, or the messages of Jesus?

A. Yes . . he taught us about health, purifications . . . he did not tell us too many secrets, though.

Q. What do you mean, secrets?

A. The things he does not tell to the masses.

Q. Do you consider yourself one of their followers?

A. Yes.

Q. What about your husband?

A. Yes, but not as much.

Q. How long ago did the crucifixion of Jesus take place?

A. Twenty years.

Q. I want you to tell me your name.

A. Diana.

Q. What is your husband's name?

A. Corinth.

Q. Let's move forward again, Diana, to another important event that takes place. (Instructions given.)

A. Peter died.

Q. How do you know that he died? Is this the talk of the people?

A. I'm at his mother's house . . . and there are people mourning.

Q. Did you become close with Peter?

A. A friend . . . I tried to help him in his work.

Q. What is the feeling toward you and those who believe as you do at this time?

A. Some people spit at us . . . some Jews have converted . . . others will convert.

Q. When you say convert, do you mean converted to Christianity?

A. Yes.

Q. Tell me more about the death of Peter and the situation right now.

A. Many people are in his mother's house in dark colors . . . I don't know the details about his death.

Q. (High-speed knowledge induction technique used at this time to bring in knowledge from the memory banks of subject's subconscious mind.) Now tell me more about the situation of Peter's death.

A. His body will not be buried according to ritual. He was tortured . . . I don't think . . . uh . . . there is nothing to take care of . . . it is out of our hands.

Q. How long have you been married at this time?

A. Twelve years.

Q. What about the situation between you and your husband? Do you have a happy life?

A. Yes.

Q. Do you have any children?

A. Yes . . . two boys.

Q. What does your husband do?

A. He is a fisherman . . . but we have traveled.

Q. Where have you traveled to?

A. It's about a day's ride to . . . Peter's mother.

Q. Do you actively try to spread the words of Jesus to the people?

A. Yes, but not as fantastically as some of the disciples.

Q. You do this in your own area then . . . to people you know?

A. Yes . . . there is a secret temple in town now . . . and I go to that.

Q. Can you worship there unmolested?

A. Yes.

Q. Are there a great many Christians now?

A. No, very few.

Q. Let's move forward again until something important happens once again. (Instructions given.)

A. We've had a fight about . . . religion.

Q. Between you and your husband?

A. Yes . . . he tends to . . . follow more the public thought of Christianity . . . which is not Christianity.

Q. What do you mean?

A. Their interpretation is they don't heed the purifications . . . either physically or mentally. . . . They're not following very much of what the Master said.

Q. Would you describe to me what the purification would include?

A. There is fasting once a week . . . once a month you fast three days or more, depending upon your present health. . . . You should eat little meat . . . you should concentrate on fruits, grains, and vegetables. . . . We should plant by the moon . . . and we should meditate at least twice, three times a day.

Q. Is this interpretation of religion a major point of dissension within your marital relationship?

A. Yes . . . he tends to pledge his life to it, but he is not willing to give to it.

Q. Let's move forward again to an important event that transpires. It can be a few minutes or a few years. Your own subconscious mind will arrive at an event in the future. (Instructions given.)

A. My eldest son is married . . . it is a pleasant occasion . . . although some soldiers in town know that there is a secret temple and that we are holding a wedding here. . . . They've been alerted to watch for us.

Q. Do you fear something happening?

A. Only for physical means.

Q. Let's move forward until something transpires. (Instructions given.)

A. Some of the soldiers have knocked down the altar . . . they've found us . . . but my son and his wife are away . . . safe.

Q. But you're still there?

A. Yes, there are about twenty of us still here.

Q. What are they going to do to you?

A. They'll probably crucify us.

Q. Is having a secret temple that much of a crime at this time?

A. Yes . . . it's against Rome. . . . There are many more Christians now in Jerusalem . . . but if the soldiers know when we are having worship . . . or when a speaker comes, they will do anything to obstruct it.

Q. Let's move forward in time until you find out what they are going to do to you. (Instructions given.)

A. I have been let go, but some of my friends haven't.

Q. Why have you been let go?

A. A man came and talked to the officials . . . and I was let go.

Q. Do you know the man?

A. I don't think so, but apparently he says he knows me.

Q. So you have not had any contact with this man.

A. No, I don't know what he looks like.

Q. What about your husband? Was he captured?

A. He got away in the beginning . . . with my son.

Q. Let's move forward in time a little way to see what has happened to your friends who were captured.

A. Some of them have been lashed many times. . . . They're trying to find out where the other secret temples are . . . they want to know our secrets . . . because they believe we have higher knowledge . . . which we do . . . but they would use it against us . . . against the people.

Q. Did you find out any more as to why you were let go?

A. I thought and I thought . . . and I have no answers. . . . It's just a miracle. . . . I don't . . . I don't know . . . I still don't know who the man was.

Q. What can you tell me about your relationship with your husband at this time?

A. We've learned not to argue about those things any more . . . they still bother us . . . but . . . I've learned to respect his . . . ah . . . his way of worship . . . and I believe he respects mine. . . . There is a strain . . . but there's nothing we can do about it except live with each other.

Q. Is there any other point of contention? Is there any

more you can tell me about the relationship you have shared?

A. Other than that it has been good . . . he's always cared for me, and I've always cared for him. . . . I've borne him two sons . . . which is highly regarded.

Q. All right, Diana, we are now going to move ahead in time again. We are going to move to the last day of your life. You will not have died or crossed over into spirit, but it will be the last day of your life. (Instructions given.)

A. I'm with a group of friends, and we're sitting within a circle . . . talking about the Master . . . and we're trying to decide how we could better spread his word . . . without antagonism from others.

Q. How old are you at this time?

A. Forty-six.

Q. How many are there in the circle?

A. Twelve . . . there are men and women . . . Corinth is there.

Q. What do you plan to do?

A. We have decided to divide up . . . and we plan to meditate early in the morning . . . all at the same time . . . wherever we are. We also have a schedule for the afternoon meditation and the evening meditation. . . . This way our prayer can go into the masses from different directions . . . and hopefully it will be more potent.

Q. Let's move forward right to the time before you experience physical death. There will be no pain and no emotion, but we will move to the time just prior to the death experience. (Instructions given.)

A. I had a vision . . . I guess it was a vision . . . and I knew that I would die soon . . . yesterday afternoon . . . a luminous figure. . . . It was reassuring me that I did well . . . and that I should give up my body without a struggle.

Q. Where are you right now?

A. I'm standing under a tree in the orchard.

Q. What is happening now?

A. A soldier . . . an official . . . coming up . . . he hit

me . . . (Subject stops talking. The subject is now carried forward into spirit and asked the following questions:)

Q. Explain more to me about what happened.

A. He hit me . . . I don't think he meant to kill me.

Q. Was he angry at you?

A. Yes . . . everybody knows who I am.

Q. Then he was angry because you are known to preach the words of the Master?

A. Yes.

Q. How were you looked upon by the majority of the people in your area?

A. The people from Rome didn't like me at all, because what we were preaching was true . . . and we had a sway over the people because we used truth . . . where the Romans have very little force any more in our land except through physical brute force. . . . Some people envied us, but they couldn't give up . . . they just couldn't give up their old ways for the new.

(End of third session)

After the session I was naturally curious about Kathy's religious background prior to becoming a yoga teacher.

"I was raised in various Protestant denominations but primarily the Congregational Church," she said. "I've always accepted the ideas, but I couldn't handle the rest of what the church meant. When I was seventeen I worked as a medic as part of a program down in Nicaragua. Instead of going to Sunday services I'd go out in a boat and meditate. My own service, I guess . . . breakaway time."

"How do your present beliefs fit in with Christianity?" I asked.

"Believing the way I do certainly does not negate Christianity. I accept Christianity, but I do not feel confined within its boundaries. Jesus was a Master, but so was Buddha. There are many others. All had important messages of truth. Those who would contend that they contradict each other are simply not interpreting their words from the proper level. Truth is universal."

"There is one extremely interesting aspect to this regression," I said. "Evidently the people were misinterpreting Jesus's teachings twenty years after His death . . . or at the least, they were not following them as He had presented them. Can you imagine what has happened to some of the original ideas over one thousand nine hundred and seventy-five years?"

"Obviously. Yet the primary message still shines through loud and clear," she responded. "Love—universal love is really the whole thing. 'Love your brother as yourself,' because we are all part of the whole. Of course the idea of loving yourself is important. You are your own temple, and this is why you should take care of your own body. 'As you sow, so shall ye reap' is karma. It couldn't be stated more clearly. If you treat others as you want to be treated, you are exercising love. If you think only positive thoughts, you are incapable of acting negatively. It's really so simple . . . hard to execute all of the time, but simple in concept."

Fourth Regression Session

July 1975

No longer looking for karmic ties or causes, I decided, for the sake of experiment, to take Kathy back to her very first incarnation upon the earth plane of existence. The trance deepened considerably. (After the regression Kathy explained that she feels she may have left her body during this time, feeling totally weightless and speaking as though she were away listening, opposed to being a part of what was transpiring. I am more inclined to think, considering the content of this portion of the regression, that she was once again experiencing a life in which she was not yet accustomed to a physical form.)

The first questions showed that she was living in a female body upon the land mass which was to be known later as Lemuria. Although there were human beings upon the earth as we would know them, she was not embodied within such a form. Her physical appearance was normal, but she explained, "Our bodies are of such a vibrational rate as to make them invisible to most living entities." When asked about what food she ate, she explained, "Our energy is of such a level that we do not need to take in food as man knows it. We get our food from the sun. It can be mentally supplied."

From the moment I began questioning Kathy about this life, her answers became perfectly structured. She spoke in a precise, calculated manner, extremely self-assured and positive. The normal regression time-lag between questions and answers was no longer there. Her response was immediate.

Q. Can you tell me your age?

A. Age is not a consideration, as such. My appearance is that of twenty-five.

Q. What do you do with your time? Do you have an occupation?

A. No. We have certain duties on the behalf of the community, in order for the community to function. Most of the duties consist of supplying thought power to the faculties, so they will run properly.

Q. Is this in the form of mind over matter, with many minds working on a single project or responsibility?

A. Yes, depending upon your level. If you're of a lower level, it takes many. For those of higher levels it would take only one or two.

Q. Is there a caste system, or a distinctive level identification system of any form within your society?

A. Yes, through the educational process, but it is not one of prejudice, it is one of practicality. It is easy to move up. It is very rare to go down a level.

Q. When you say education, do you mean a textbook education or spiritual evolution?

A. Spiritual evolution. We are very much interested in

the abilities of the mind for communication and positive manipulation. We're having some trouble with a few who, having achieved the higher levels, are using the knowledge for negative processing.

Q. Do you know where you came from? What of your teaching of your own history and background . . . what are you taught?

A. We are pure consciousness. When the sun comes to a particular angle with the stars, we manifest into a vibration allowing us to solidify ourselves, to learn about our consciousness, how diverse it can be. To learn about creativity.

Q. Are you trapped within a physical form, or are you free to leave your body at will?

A. I can leave and return at will.

Q. Why did you choose to experience in a physical form on the earth plane?

A. There are sections of the consciousness that needed to be formed . . . to go through the creative action, to learn to be responsible for that creative action.

Q. Do you fear entrapment within the physical plane?

A. No.

Q. Are many of those there with you also experiencing life on the earth plane for the first time?

A. Many are, yes.

Q. For what reason would you leave your body? Why would you return to the spiritual levels?

A. We go back for energy. We go through various levels before returning to the source. On each level as we leave the earth plane, there are elders stationed for our coming. They verify what we have done and what we have learned. Then we go to the source for the energy necessary to continue our life within physical form.

Q. Do you have problems or fears in the physical body?

A. I'm still having a little difficulty in perfectly controlling my body. I have found that I still have to consciously will my body to move at times.

Q. Is this a normal situation for those just crossing over into the physical form?

A. For some it is; others may have difficulty in working with any of the five physical senses. I can normally move well. It is only upon occasion that I have delayed reactions.

Q. Where do you live?

A. A building of high vibration which we mentally created. It completely protects us from the heat or the cold or the rain.

Q. Then you have carried with you the spiritual ability to mentally create a material object or an environment?

A. Yes.

Q. Individually or as a group?

A. As I explained before, we are on different levels. Your capabilities depend upon your level.

Q. Are there accidents or sickness where you are now?

A. Accidents occur when someone's thought is not consistent. When he breaks his concentration level and allows his energy to scatter, yet we are presently at a level where we cannot be harmed physically.

Q. Do you retain conscious knowledge of the spiritual realms as well as the earth plane?

A. Yes, we have to check in at the different levels. For some it is once a day, for others it is every several days. This is to help us keep our ties and to avoid being caught within a lower vibration from which we could become a gross manifestation.

Q. Being trapped within this lower vibration could mean entrapment upon the earth, necessitating a cycle of reincarnation to evolve back to the source—is this correct?

A. Yes. You would no longer be able to consciously leave the physical, except in rare situations, until physical death.

Q. What about physical death upon the plane of existence you are now experiencing?

A. Our bodies do not wear out. We keep them totally rejuvenated. We can make a conscious decision to serve the elders on the spiritual planes, giving up our physical bodies.

Q. Is there contact at this time with any other lands? Are there settlements of people who know only physical existence?

A. There are those of gross manifestation. We try to send them information and guidance. They do not know we exist. Their body rate is of a lower pace.

Q. Do you know of any contact with outer space? Not the spiritual realms, but physical beings from other planets?

A. There are many, although there is little contact, for we are yet small. We contact them mentally. Some of the races have manifested in such a gross state you can only use physical means, such as sending objects to their planet or their sphere. They have built up such barriers in their mind so as to become incapable of recognizing incoming thoughts.

Q. How do you send an object to another planet?

A. By thought. We mentally create the object, and we designate the destination. We give it the power to go there.

Q. Would you describe your present state of being as half physical and half spiritual?

A. Yes.

(End of fourth session)

Much of what was received in the last portion of this regression was new to both Kathy and me. Some of the concepts are collaborated by the Edgar Cayce readings, but Kathy had never read them. A few old esoteric books have covered some of these theories, but they are not well known. There is no doubt that Kathy was in the deepest possible hypnotic sleep, and upon being awakened, she was as amazed as I about what we had just received.

"I think you got trapped on the earth plane," I said as she sat up and began rubbing her hands.

"So do I," she responded. "A gross manifestation in the flesh! Why didn't I stay where I had it made?"

Melinda and Tom

IN JULY 1975 I CONDUCTED A SMALL GROUP REGRESSION session in the home of financial columnist Bob Rosefsky. The Rosefskys are old friends, and Bob's wife, Linda Sue, has been a constant collaborator and supportive friend throughout all the experiments and research work conducted over the years. When I should be reading new, unfamiliar material, she's been the one to hand me the book. When I have gotten off the track, she's been right there with constructive criticism. Her book club has often served as a research laboratory for the development of techniques and for experimental sessions.

On this particular evening several of her friends were invited over to experience regression and aid me in the search for interesting cases of man/woman relationships from the past that helped to explain the present. Fourteen women and one man, a local Scottsdale doctor, had gathered to take part in the session.

A few of the women remained in their chairs, but the majority made themselves comfortable, lying prone upon the floor. Once hypnosis was induced, I gave them the following instructions:

"I want you to move way back in time, to a previous lifetime, and I want your subconscious mind to choose a life in which you have known someone who is very important presently to you in this life. As I guide you and ask you questions, I want you to see the situations very vividly, to understand them, and to answer the questions to yourself in your own mind."

When the session was completed, I found that all but one woman had received at least some form of visual impressions and knowledge about a prior life. It was a first-time experience for most of those present, and I found several good subjects within the group.

There is usually considerable excitement and surprise among the participants immediately following the awakening procedure. They are left with the suggestion to remember everything they have experienced and to awaken refreshed and relaxed, feeling joyful and full of energy. I normally allow the group to talk among themselves for several minutes, before beginning to question them individually about what they have re-experienced.

Several had found themselves in past situations with someone other than their present-day husband or lover. In one case it was with a brother, with another a parent, and a couple saw themselves with close friends. A few had received strong impressions and pictures but could not fit them together with present relationship ties.

When I asked Melinda, a very pretty twenty-eight-year-old, what she had received, she responded, "I don't believe it, but I saw it so clearly. My own son had another man and myself executed. We were living in Spain, and he had us shot."

Before awakening the group, I had taken them into a superconscious state of hypnosis and had instructed them to receive understanding as to how their past and present were linked. "Are you aware of any present-day ties with this prior life?" I asked.

"Yes, my husband of today was the man who was executed with me."

I had planned on doing a single regression, so that those present could observe the verbal questions and answers in directed individual hypnosis. I asked Melinda if she would be willing to be the subject, and she agreed. While the rest of the group had coffee, Melinda and I went out by the swimming pool to talk about her background.

"Are you a friend of Linda Sue's?" I asked.

"No, I've never met her before tonight," she said. "I came with Mary, just out of curiosity."

"Do you have any understanding of reincarnation, karma, and metaphysics?"

"Very, very little. Mary has talked about it a few times, but I don't know enough to begin to form any opinion one way or another. Yet I certainly can't explain what I just experienced."

"Do you presently belong to a particular church denomination?" I asked.

"Oh, yes, I'm Lutheran, and we attend church."

I explained to Melinda that I would like to ask her some further personal questions if she wouldn't mind answering them, because it would be helpful in making the individual regression more meaningful. She was very open and easy in her conversation, answering my questions frankly. Melinda is employed as an assistant to a veterinarian. Her husband, Tom, is thirty-one and works as a wholesale lumber salesman. They have been married for three months and are extremely happy. A previous marriage of three years' duration had been "incredibly bad from the very beginning," to quote her.

"My first husband and I were separated while I was pregnant," she said. "I had horrible premonitions during that time. I felt that my child was evil. I couldn't shake the feeling that the child was bad, that there was something terribly wrong about the entire situation. The baby was born dead."

"When were you divorced?" I asked.

"Right after that. I knew it would never work, and our relationship wasn't right . . . for many reasons and none at all. It's hard to put into words, but I knew from the moment we first got married."

Melinda was already conditioned in hypnosis, so the trance was induced very quickly. She lay on the floor with her head resting on a pillow, the others present in the room gathered around in a circle, a few feet away.

Melinda

First Individual Session

July 1975

I now instructed Melinda to return to the Spanish life-time. "I want you to go back to the lifetime in Spain in which you and your present husband, Tom, were previously together. It will be the time of your very first meeting." (Instructions given.)

Q. What do you see and what are you doing?

A. I'm outdoors . . . he's helping me into a cart with hay on the back . . . and I see an old woman chasing me. . . . He's helping me into the cart.

Q. Why is the old woman after you?

A. I don't know.

Q. Describe yourself to me.

A. I'm very young, I have blond hair in pigtails and I'm trying to get away from the old woman . . . and he's helping me into the cart.

Q. All right, let's move forward in time one hour. (Instructions given.)

A. There is a lake, forest . . . trees, we're just driving by in the cart . . . just riding in the cart with the young boy who picked me up.

Q. Did you know this boy before?

A. No.

Q. What is he saying to you?

A. Nothing, we're just riding along.

Q. Do you know now about the old woman who was chasing you? Think about it and explain the situation to me.

A. She's my grandmother . . . my grandmother. . . . I don't like her.

Q. How old are you at this time?
A. Seven.

As I moved Melinda forward in time, we discovered she was living a very poor life in a town named Trinidad. She was alone and existed primarily by stealing food and sleeping in the streets. She saw the boy in the cart several times while growing up and again at twenty-three, when he was a soldier marching through the streets of the town. Later she saw herself working in a hospital; the same young man had been wounded and she was helping to take care of him. Upon recovery he returned to the army.

Q. I now want you to move to the last day of your life. You will not have died or crossed over into spirit, but it will be the last day of your life. (Instructions given.)
A. I'm an older woman . . . in prison . . . in debtors' prison.
Q. Why are you in prison?
A. Stealing.
Q. Did you ever see the young man again after he left the hospital?
A. No . . . I wanted to . . . no.
Q. But you felt very drawn to him?
A. Yes.
Q. I want to know your name.
A. Julie Anne.

It was now obvious to me that Melinda had jumped a lifetime on me. Either she had misunderstood the instructions or her subconscious mind felt she needed once again to tap in on this lifetime, as is sometimes the case.

I did not ask her the name of the country she was in at the time, but later research showed numerous Trinidads in the United States and eleven in Central and South America, in addition to the island. These countries were possessions of Spain. There is presently no town by that name in Spain, according to the World Atlas, but it is evidently a common Spanish name, so there may be a very small town there now, or it could have existed at that time. The Spanish aspect of the lifetime may have confused my original instructions.

I decided to move Melinda forward to the next lifetime that she and Tom were together, if indeed such a life existed.

This time she saw herself and Tom as childhood friends at the age of nine. "He's always bothering me," she said. "I pretend not to like him, but I do." I then carried her forward to the age of eighteen.

Q. What do you see and what are you doing at this time?

A. I have to get married . . . my mother is making me get married.

Q. Is the person you are going to marry the little boy you were playing with before?

A. No, to somebody I don't want to marry.

Q. Why is your mother forcing you to get married?

A. Money.

Q. What city are you living in now?

A. Madrid.

Q. Was this marriage arranged by both your parents?

A. Yes . . . I don't love him . . . he is a cruel person. . . . My parents want the money.

Q. Let's move forward to the actual marriage ceremony, if this takes place. (Instructions given.)

A. Married in a huge mansion . . . not a church. . . . I see many blank faces . . . blank empty faces.

Q. But you did marry this man?

A. I married him.

Q. Let's move forward in time again to something important that happens in the future. (Instructions given.)

A. We're riding through the town . . . I see the boy I used to know. . . . He's grown up now . . . I love him . . . he's a peasant . . . I'm very wealthy, but I hate my husband.

Q. How long have you been married now?

A. Five years.

Q. Do you have any children at this time?

A. No.

Q. What is your life like? I want you to describe the relationship between yourself and your husband.

A. I hate him . . . I hate him . . . I don't want any relationship with him . . . I don't even acknowledge his existence.

Q. What are his feelings toward you?

A. Oh . . . he's very, very cold. . . . I'm a showpiece . . . that's all. . . . He doesn't care.

Q. What about the boy you do love? Has there been any recent contact between the two of you?

A. No . . . but I'm going to see him.

Q. If you do see him, I want you to move forward to the time of this meeting. (Instructions given.)

A. It's a very cold . . . rainy night . . . I'm finally going to see him . . . where he lives. . . . Very old . . . ground floor . . . big fireplace . . . very warm . . . very warm. . . .

Q. What is happening?

A. We're holding each other.

Q. Then he feels very much the same way toward you?

A. Yes.

Q. I want to move forward now, one month in time. (Instructions given.) I now want you to tell me what has happened within the month, between you and the young man you love.

A. We're going to leave together . . . going to run away. . . . We love each other. It's so hard to get away . . . so hard . . . so hard to get away.

Q. Why?

A. Too many obstacles . . . my husband is an evil person.

Q. Does he have any idea that the affair is going on?

A. No.

Q. Are you and the young man now lovers?

A. Yes . . . oh, yes.

Q. (I now attempted to move Melinda forward to the time she and her lover left, but such an escape did not take place in the following years.) Tell me about what has happened.

A. Several years have gone by . . . several. . . . I've had his child.

Q. But you are still married to your husband?

A. Yes, I never left.

Q. Does your husband feel that the child is his?

A. Yes. . . . (There is hatred in the subject's voice.) Yes.

Q. Are you continuing the affair with the man you do love?

A. Yes . . . we're going to leave with the child.

Q. What has blocked you from leaving before this time?

A. I don't know . . . I just don't know . . . fear him. . . . I don't understand why we didn't leave sooner . . . I just don't know."

Q. All right, if you actually do leave, I want to move forward to that time. (Instructions given.)

A. He has a huge cart . . . we're going . . . my son . . .

Q. How old is your son at this time?

A. Five years old. . . . My son is just like my husband . . . he doesn't want to go. . . . He's not his son, but he's just like him.

Q. Do you feel then that your husband has had a great influence on the child?

A. Yes.

Q. How old are you at this time?

A. Twenty-nine.

Q. What has your relationship with your husband been like for the last few years?

A. I hate him . . . I hate him . . . he disgusts me.

Q. Has there been any physical violence?

A. No . . . nothing physical . . . mental violence.

Q. What is his occupation?

A. Dignitary. . . . I see him in his long coat . . . stepping all over people . . . dishonest.

Q. All right, now you are leaving with your lover. Does he have a plan?

A. Farming . . . and . . . we have to get very far away. . . . We're going to Portugal . . . that's . . . we're going to live there . . . we're very happy.

Q. Let's move forward in time a year. (Instructions given.)

A. We're standing on the front porch . . . we have a little house . . . it's warm and breezy, very nice.

Q. Do you have a farm now?

A. Yes . . . we're very happy.

Q. What about your son? Is he there with you?

A. Yes . . . but he doesn't accept the situation. . . . I don't like him.

Q. You're about thirty years of age now, living in Portugal. Have you gotten a divorce from your husband?

A. No . . . oh, no . . . we're just living together.

Q. Have you ever had any further contact with your husband?

A. No.

Although I desired to question Melinda further, she had been in a trance for a long time, so I started to bring the session to an end.

Q. I now want to move forward in time again to the very last day of your life. You will not have died, or crossed over into spirit, but it will be the last day of your life and I want you to tell me what you are experiencing at this time. (Instructions given.)

A. We're being executed . . . my son has taken over his father's . . . my first husband's position. . . . There is a revolution . . . we're peasants . . . they're killing many people . . . they're having us executed.

Q. Who is having you executed?

A. My son . . . he's rotten . . . my husband had too much influence upon him . . . he's rotten.

Q. How old are you at this time?

A. I'm old . . . so old . . . I'm ready to die . . . very, very old. . . . I did what I wanted to do.

Q. Did you ever have any other children?

A. No.

Q. Is the man you've lived with all these years there with you now?

A. Yes.

Q. Is there anything more you can tell me about the situation?

A. I see us holding each other.

Q. What year is it now?

A. 1869.

Q. How will you be executed?

A. They're going to shoot us.

I now moved Melinda beyond what she was experiencing, and up into the higher-self, superconscious area of her own mind.

Q. From this perspective, Melinda, you have the ability to answer many questions about what we have just re-examined. I first want you to tell me if the man you loved and lived with in Spain is your present husband, Tom, in this life.

A. Yes. . . . (Subject begins to cry, and strong calming suggestions are given.) I don't want to go into these realms without him. (It was explained that she was perfectly safe and could return at any time that she desired to do so. That Tom was with her there in spirit. She then relaxed and proceeded to answer my next question.)

Q. Have you had any contact in your present life with the man who was your husband in the Spanish lifetime?

A. Yes . . . my first husband in this life . . . but the child in Spain . . . . he was just like my husband, though he was Tom's child . . . but he looked just like my husband . . . acted just like . . . (Subject began to get very upset again, so I created an artificial mental environment and spent several minutes relaxing her and implanting positive suggestions.)

(End of first session)

There were obviously many unanswered questions, so I made arrangements with Melinda to return to Scottsdale in a week for a second regression session. In the meantime research uncovered some interesting facts.

HISTORIC FOLLOW-UP NOTES:

The time period of the regression was during and immediately following the Spanish Inquisition, a period of religious bigotry and fanatical intolerance, resulting in massive executions. Although the feared tribunal was finally dissolved, individual tribunals continued to carry on a shadowlike existence for many years, executing heretics and creating widespread fear. As the Inquisition ended, the country degenerated into a period of civil war. Spain continued to be the most turbulent country in Europe, with continual and meaningless revolutions, court intrigues, and general lawlessness until 1875. Although Melinda was in Portugal in later life, the situation there was nearly identical to that of Spain.

The next time we met was at Melinda and Tom's home in Scottsdale. Tom and a woman friend of Melinda's were also there. We talked about the first session and her reactions to what she had experienced. "I couldn't get it out of my mind all week—it just kept bothering me," she said. "The first three days were the worst—it gave me a headache I couldn't shake."

Because of her reactions, I decided it would be better not to take her back into the Spanish lifetime right away.

Melinda

Second Regression Session

August 1975

Hypnosis induced and regression preparation completed. I then gave her the following instructions: "I want you now to return to a lifetime between the Spanish life and your present life if there was another incarnation

between your death in 1869 and your birth as Melinda.
I want you to return to an important situation that
transpired during that last life. If there has been no other
lifetime between the lives I've mentioned, on the count of
eleven you will speak up and tell me so. (Instructions
given.)

Q. What do you see and what are you doing at this time?
A. It's very confusing . . . there's a woman . . . I seem
to be indoors, but I'm on a boat. . . . I feel like I'm
under the boat yet. . . .
Q. Is there anything you can communicate to me about
where you are?
A. It's a huge boat . . . I just see this boat . . . this
woman . . . she has a baby . . . but before I felt like
I was under it . . . like I was drowning. . . . My
lungs were filling up with water.
Q. What else can you tell me?
A. I can't find my way . . . I don't know . . . it's very dark
. . . I'm on my back holding onto the bottom. . . .
(The subject starts to become upset.)
Q. Let's let go of this, I want you now to move back-
ward in time just a few weeks. (Instructions given.)
A. I see a big city . . . everybody is very gay . . . con-
fetti is coming down on the streets.
Q. Is there anyone there with you now?
A. No.
Q. What are you doing?
A. I'm laughing and dancing . . . I'm very gay.
Q. Do you know any of the people who are there in the
streets?
A. No . . . but I see my mother . . . it's very strange . . .
I . . . ah . . . I feel that I am laughing and dancing
. . . yet . . . I see my mother . . . but I'm not separate
. . . we're not separate people, we're one person.
. . . I don't know.
Q. What is the reason for the gaiety?
A. Parade . . . ah . . .
Q. How old are you at this time?
A. I don't think I have any age.

Q. You must have an age, and on the count of three you
will tell me your age. One—two—three.

A. Twenty-three.

Q. Let's move forward in time just one day. (Instructions given.) What do you see and what are you
experiencing at this time?

A. I'm sad.

Q. Why are you sad?

A. I'm not sure . . . I'm dressed in a brown woolen
shawl. . . . Very sad.

Q. Is there anyone there with you now?

A. No . . . I'm sitting in the kitchen.

Q. Describe the environment for me.

A. Everything is very plain . . . I'm sitting at the table
on a wooden chair. . . . It's all very dull . . . apartment . . . three floors up.

Q. Does anyone live there with you?

A. No one.

Q. Where is your mother at this time?

A. I . . . ah . . . I still see my mother sitting at the
table . . . there's only one person there. (Subject
seems very confused.)

Q. All right, don't question that. The sadness you are
feeling. I want you to understand the reason for this
sadness and communicate it to me. On the count of
three your mind will clear and you will fully understand. One—two—three.

A. I feel sad for my mother . . . (Subject starts to cry
and calming suggestions are given.) She's pregnant
. . . with . . . with me.

Q. Why does she feel sad? Shouldn't this be a happy
occasion?

A. No.

Q. Isn't your mother married at this time?

A. No . . . I feel so sad for her.

Q. You are there then, in the proximity of your mother,
but you're still in spirit, is that correct?

A. She's carrying me . . . I'm sad for her, but I am where
I want to be and I'm not going to leave.

Q. Let's move forward in time, to the time your mother

books passage upon a boat, if this does transpire. (Instructions given.)

A. I see her buying a ticket, she is going to go away.

Q. Is she leaving because she wants to get away, to hide from friends and relatives?

A. Yes . . . but she is very much alone . . . she doesn't really have anyone. She's just going away . . . she just wants to go away.

Additional questioning revealed that the ship her mother sailed on sank in the Atlantic and most of its passengers were lost.

The situation was now quite obvious, so I moved Melinda back into the present, but instructed her to remain in a deep hypnotic sleep. Being hesitant at this time to return her to the Spanish life, I decided to take her once more into the superconscious area of her mind. (Instructions given.)

Q. Tell me what you are experiencing at this time.

A. It's very bright light . . . so bright I can barely see.

Q. Are you perceiving any colors?

A. White and sort of an orange.

Q. All right, now you're in an easy, warm environment and I want you to answer a few questions for me. From this perspective you have the power and ability to do this. Is it possible, in the past life we just examined, that Tom was to have been your mother?

A. No . . . I was his mother at one time. It wasn't very long ago because I see myself in . . . ah . . . early 1900s in the United States.

Q. Any particular part of this country?

A. I see Iowa.

Q. Do you know of any other incarnations that you have shared? Any other lifetimes you have been together?

A. Yes . . . we were babies . . . little babies . . . I can see us playing together. . . . I don't know when it . . . we grew up together . . . very close, but we didn't grow to adulthood together. They took him away from me . . . oh . . . (Subject begins to become very upset;

tears are running down her cheeks. Strong calming suggestions are given, but she continues to cry, so I command her to block the pictures and the memories.)

Q. We are moving on to other questions at this time, completely forgetting what we just discussed. Do you know of any other lifetimes, other than those we already know about, in which you and Tom have known each other?

A. (There is a several-minute pause in which the subject attempts to avoid answering.) I want to say no . . . I want to say no . . . there actually is, but I want to say no.

Q. Is this something that would be very painful to examine?

A. Yes.

Q. Would you prefer not to discuss it at this time?

A. It makes me very sad . . . I . . . uh . . . there has been an old woman following me around all my different lives, and I don't want . . . I can't say any more about it. . . . She's always following me . . . I'm afraid of her. . . . She's here right now . . . she was here when we first started, and she was there the first night at Linda Sue's house.

I had intended to ask Melinda additional questions about the Spanish lifetime we scanned in the first session, but the presence of an unknown entity changed the situation. The first step was to intensify the protection around the subject. "All right, we are now going to block this entity. We absolutely have the power and the ability to block her. The white light around your body is totally protective . . . totally protective . . . now feel it, and once more I want you to see the golden light coming down from above. Believe me, I know exactly what I am talking about. . . . See the golden light of God coming down from above, stronger and more intense than it has ever been before. It is now entering the top of your head, feel it flowing down into your body and manifesting around the area of your heart. Now see it in your mind and feel it emanating from the area around your heart. It is totally surrounding your body . . . your body is totally surrounded by a protective aura of white light. . . . See it in your mind and feel it, and thus it becomes reality. You are totally protected, and only the influence of your own guides, or Masters, can now have any influence upon you in any way.

"If we are now uncovering the presence of an entity that has been a problem to you in the past, this can be eliminated." (Talking now directly to the old woman.) "If you are here and have attached yourself in any way to Melinda, you are very unaware. If you have been harmful to this woman in the past, you must now understand that you can be blocked. From this moment on, Melinda will be able to block your influence at all times, for she now knows how to protect herself. You are only hurting yourself. You must realize that you are dead. . . . You are dead, and you are obviously tormenting yourself. . . . There is absolutely no reason for you to go on with such torment. . . . All you have to do is realize that you can let go of the torment. You can rise above it right now. You have probably been contacted in the past by more highly evolved entities who have offered to help you, but you haven't listened. You must listen now, for if you do not, you will be taken away. You have seen glimpses of light in the past, and you must now know that all you have to do is to go to the light and you will find help to rise above your present situation of torment. You must let go of the past, and you will be free of the torment and confusion. Regardless of what may have taken place between you and this woman in another time and another place, you can be free to find peace if you choose to do so.

"I am now calling upon the help of Melinda's own guides, I am invoking the aid of higher Masters. I am calling you, requesting your aid. I also want you to call them, Melinda. I want you to ask for their help. They have the ability to help you if you ask for their aid. You call them with your mind and they will come. They have the ability to show the old woman the proper pathway, and if she will not listen, they can take her away. This problem may be lifetimes old, and it is time to eliminate it . . . it is time to remove it. Call in your guides and Masters and ask them for the help."

(Several minutes pass.)

Q. Melinda, I now want you to speak up and tell me if you still feel the presence of the old woman, or if you are receiving any visual impressions.
A. No.

I wanted Melinda to remember everything that happened, so before awaking her, I gave a posthypnotic command to remember the entire regression, and to use the technique we had just completed if she ever needed it in the future.

(End of second session)

Upon awakening, she was still obviously shaken by what she had experienced. "She was there the first time too. I tried to ignore it, but she was always there, and it made me nervous. What was that all about?"

"I wish I knew for sure," I answered. "I've experienced the presence of other entities myself while in trance, so I know the feeling, but this may be much more complicated than that. This form of a very minor exorcism has worked successfully in the past, and we can explore it further in the future if you desire to do so, but we may have solved it tonight. One thing is for sure, if you feel fearful of the presence, it is negative. It could have been with you for thousands of years, and we have stumbled across it accidentally through the regressions. Of course I don't believe that anything like that is accidental; it may simply be that you have risen above a past situation karmicly, and it was time to remove an old weight."

The rest of the evening was spent discussing similar cases and the world of metaphysics in general. Both Melinda and Tom were extremely interested in the new way of thinking that seemed to be flooding in upon their lives.

The second regression had introduced more questions

than answers, and the important information from the Spanish lifetime was still unknown. We made a date to do a third session at their home one week later.

Melinda

Third Regression Session

August 1975

Six people were in attendance as observers in Melinda and Tom's living room for the third session. Melinda was obviously nervous about the idea of running into the old woman again. We had mitigated the effects she experienced after the first session, with strong posthypnotic suggestions in the second, so she did not fear the mental anguish or headaches, but the element of fear remained with respect to the presence of a negative entity. She felt the old woman had blocked her from using the self-releasing mechanism when she had desired to do so. I decided to intensify every aspect of protection and to invoke another form of release. This seemed to satisfy Melinda, for she was as anxious as I to find answers in the past.

Hypnosis induced, preparation completed, and protectory measures introduced.

Q. Do you feel the presence of the old woman there with you at this time?

A. No.

Q. Do you feel relaxed and at ease?

A. Yes.

Q. You are now in a deep hypnotic sleep, completely relaxed and completely at ease, both mentally and physically. You are aware of the knowledge we have attained about your past, and you know of your present life. I want to know if you can tell me any more about the old woman, if she has been with you in many lifetimes.

A. I feel she has, but not any more. She is not here now.

Q. All right, I now want to go back in time to the lifetime you and Tom shared in Spain, to the lifetime in which you were executed. I want to return to a few weeks before the actual execution. You will return as an observer, without pain and without emotion. (Instructions given.) Tell me now, what do you see and what are you doing?

A. We're surrounded . . . a huge courtyard . . . it's like a prison . . . huge walls all around . . . there are many people.

Q. Are you free to move around in the courtyard, or are you imprisoned within a cell?

A. No, we're free to move around, but we can't go outside the walls.

Q. Why are you here? Have you committed some kind of crime?

A. There's a revolution, it's a religious revolution. I'm a little confused . . . there are the Protestants and the Catholics. . . . I don't know.

Q. Did your son have anything to do with your being arrested?

A. He doesn't know that he's my son . . . I'm an old woman.

Q. How do you know that he is your son?

A. I've always known . . . I've always known what he was doing . . . and where he was.

Q. Did he leave home at an early age?

A. He was taken away.

Q. Why?

A. My husband had him taken away.

Q. Then your husband found out where you were?

A. Yes . . . he was taken at eleven . . . eleven years old.

Q. I want to know your name.

A. Maria.

Q. What is the name of the man you love?

A. Jules.

Q. Have you and Jules had a happy life together?

A. Yes . . . very happy.

Q. Did you remain on the land, farming?

A. Yes.

Q. Have you ever had any further contact with your husband at all?

A. No, he's the one that took my son away.

Q. Was there no contact when he took your son? How was this done?

A. We were working in the fields . . . and this army . . . they just came and took him away.

Q. You were not harmed in any way at that time?

A. No.

Q. Is your husband in any way responsible for the situation you now find yourself in, in prison?

A. Well . . . indirectly. He raised my son . . . he's rotten.

Q. What was your son like before he was taken?

A. He was just a bad seed . . . we should have left him . . . he . . .

Q. Let's let go of this, and once again we are going to move back to the present and up into the all-knowing perspective of the higher-self, superconscious mental realms. (Instructions given.)

Q. I'm looking for insight through the answers you will now be able to give me. I desire knowledge that will tie the past and present together if such ties in reality do exist. I now want you to tell me about the child who was born to you in this life. The child you felt was evil prior to his stillbirth.

A. He was evil . . . the same soul that was my son in the Spanish lifetime . . . he had to die, because he was responsible for our deaths . . . it couldn't happen this time.

Q. Is there any more you can tell me and thus yourself about how these lifetimes tie together? I want you to blow out the past and rise above it.

A. There is . . . some connection between . . . my husband was trying to use him to destroy us, and he had to die.

Q. Do you feel the individual who was your husband in

the Spanish lifetime and your first husband in this life
was working against you in your present incarnation?
A. Yes . . . (Very vehement.) Yes . . . but I overcame
the evil of it all . . . he was trying to destroy me again.

The subject was given strong suggestions and instructions
for protection, then awakened.

(End of third session)

"Remember and use the protection, Melinda, there is
no way anyone from the lower astral can affect you unless
you allow them to do so."

"I really feel better now," she said. "There is still a
lot I don't understand, but what I do certainly makes
sense."

AFTERNOTE:

I would like to have questioned Melinda more about
the "evil child," but her emotional reactions to this subject
were extremely intense, resulting in tears and the inability
to communicate. In my opinion, a karmic tie between
her and the identity she experienced as her son started
well before the lifetimes we covered in these regressions.
It probably resulted from a negative situation that was
given so much power at the time that it carried forward
over the centuries.

On several occasions I have worked with well-known
psychics in an attempt to establish the exact nature of
such a problem. Sometimes we succeeded and sometimes
not. A hypnotized subject may simply refuse to relive a
horrible event from his own past, often moving right up
to it but unwilling to re-examine it, or reacting in such a
violent manner as to warrant continuing inadvisable.

Jane and Don

JANE AND DON ARE A MODERN-DAY LOVE STORY. THERE is nothing particularly glamorous about their present lives, but they are a living example of the durability of love and its capacity to rise above numerous problems. Both were drawn thousands of miles, from different parts of the country, to meet again in Phoenix, Arizona . . . for their fourth lifetime together.

Jane came to one of our early experimental regression sessions of about twenty-five people. She was new to the Pheonix area and was there not out of any interest on her own but because her date was intrigued with what we were doing.

She was an attractive but slightly overweight girl of thirty and had no knowledge of hypnosis or reincarnation. She did not believe she could be hypnotized, much less regressed.

Also attending the session was a good friend of mine, a thirty-two-year-old commercial artist named Don Johnson. Don had come alone but had met Jane on a previous occasion and seemed especially attentive to her as I saw them together during the course of the evening.

I started the session with my standard twenty-minute introductory talk, explaining hypnosis in general—what it could and couldn't do. I then hypnotized the group. The majority of those attending went into a trance. Jane was among them. She was obviously a very good subject, her body relaxed correctly, and she passed all the tests, so she was naturally one of the people I asked to regress individually.

Jane

First Regression Session

October 1972

Hypnosis induced and regression preparation completed. The following instructions were then given: "You will return to your previous lifetime, the lifetime you lived before the present life you are now living. On the count of eleven you will be in this past life at the age of ten." (One to eleven count and instructions completed.)

Q. What do you see and what are you doing?
A. There's a windmill . . . I'm outdoors . . . trees.
Q. How are you dressed?
A. Pants.
Q. Where do you live?
A. Amsterdam.
Q. Whom do you live with?
A. My mother and father.
Q. Do you have any brothers and sisters?
A. No.
Q. Can you tell me what year it is?
A. 1801.
Q. You can tell me your name. I want to know your name.
A. Hans.

At this point in the regression the subject was moved forward in time five years to the age of fifteen. She saw herself as a male walking through the city streets from classes, carrying an armload of books. It was established that Hans's father was a teacher in a private Catholic school. His mother was a housewife. When told that he had the ability to speak to me in his native language, Dutch, he easily did so. (This is unusual in regression, for although the subject can usually understand his former language when he hears it spoken by someone else in the room, very few trance subjects can speak it again. Jane had no conscious ties with the Netherlands and knew nothing of the Dutch language.) The subject was now moved forward another five years to the age of twenty.

Q. What do you see and what are you doing?
A. I'm tall . . . I'm wearing a uniform. A blue coat and white pants.
Q. Are you in the navy?
A. Yes.
Q. What is your job in the navy?
A. Paperwork . . . I've never been to sea.

The subject was moved forward another five years to the age of twenty-five.

Q. Where are you now, Hans? Tell me what is happening.
A. My heart . . . oh . . . I have pain . . . I've been hurt . . . I'm wounded.
Q. How were you wounded?
A. Shot . . . by a gun.
Q. Were you in a battle?
A. Yes.
Q. Are you at sea now?
A. Yes.
Q. Is anyone helping you?
A. The captain . . . he's reading to me. (Subject is showing intense anguish. Suggestions given to calm down and feel no pain.)
Q. What is he reading to you?
A. A psalm.

Further questioning revealed that Hans was moved to his bunk on the ship but soon died from the wounds. In discussing the situation after the session, Jane said that the man who shot Hans was not in a uniform. She felt that Hans was a part of a coastal patrol and the enemy were looters or pirates.

HISTORIC FOLLOW-UP NOTE:

A check of several history books showed that the Barbary pirates and the Atlantic slave traders were a major problem in the waters between England and the Netherlands at exactly this time, and the Dutch government did indeed maintain a strong coastal patrol along their ocean boundaries.

Before awakening Jane, I carried her through the death experience and into spirit.

Q. Tell me what you feel. What you are experiencing at this time?

A. I feel peaceful . . . there is a haze.

Q. Is there anyone there with you?

A. A few . . . they have no faces.

Q. You have the ability to look back upon this life you have just come out of. I want you now to answer some questions about your life as Hans. Was there any woman of importance in your life?

A. Gretchen.

Q. Did you intend to marry her?

A. No.

Q. Were you in love with her?

A. Yes.

Q. Why didn't you marry her?

A. Because . . . I was going to sea.

Q. All right, I want you to let go of this now, and you will move forward in time until you find yourself in a different situation. (Instructions given.)

A. I don't like them . . . I don't like the feeling. (The subject shows fear in her voice. She was obviously going through the lower astral planes, which are the discarnate levels of the lowest vibrations. Souls who have lowered their level of consciousness while living often find themselves trapped within this dark, cold, and fearful environment for a time after experiencing metamorphosis. Contacts with ghosts and negative entities can usually be explained by an understanding of this confusing entrapment. Instructions were given to move the subject beyond this level.)

A. It is like the sun on top of a mountain . . . snow. . . .
Q. Do you like it there?
A. Yes.
Q. Have you created this place, with the power of your own mind?
A. No, I only exist.
Q. How did you find this place?
A. I breathed.

It was established through maneuvering in time and space that she had been contacted by a Master who had explained she would spend time learning and in seclusion, and that in time she would find "a baby in the sun." I now attempted to move Jane forward to learn more about the spiritual realms, but the following questions and answers showed that although she was still in spirit, she had returned to the earth plane.

Q. What are you experiencing at this time?
A. A little girl is there . . . she's a baby.
Q. Where are you now?
A. I'm looking at the baby.
Q. Can you tell me where you are? Do you know where you are?
A. Yes . . . my home.

A series of questions and answers established that Jane was still in spirit. No one else could see her; she walked through objects, opposed to walking around them. She said that she was free to go anywhere she wanted to go, but that it made her feel good to be there; she didn't want to go anywhere else. The place she presently found herself was not the home she had known as Hans.

Q. What has drawn you here?
A. The baby.
Q. What do you feel toward the baby?
A. I want to be the baby.
Q. You want to be reborn?
A. I want to be *that* baby.

Through additional questioning it was established that her own soul re-entered the baby's body, that she was watching her present self, Jane, as a newborn infant. More than one hundred earth years had passed since Hans had died at sea.

(End of first session)

I was interested in following up on the first session with Jane, and Don was interested in her in other ways. They started dating and became quite involved shortly after the evening of regressions. Don and I talked about doing another session in private, and a few weeks later the three of us met at my home to search for further information about Hans.

Jane

Second Regression Session

November 1972

The hypnotic trance was induced. Jane is an unusual subject in that she totally freezes in her position while in hypnosis. If a hand is slightly raised when she goes under, it remains in that position, absolutely unmoving throughout the trance. This naturally would be an absolute impossibility for anyone not in a hypnotic trance.

Regression conditioning was completed, and Jane was instructed to return to the lifetime as Hans at the age of twenty.

Q. Tell me what you see and what you are doing.
A. I'm in a room. . . . I'm in the military.
Q. How long have you been in the military?
A. A year.
Q. Why did you join?
A. I love the sea.
Q. All right, Hans, I now want you to tell me your name . . . your last name.
A. I have two names . . . K-r-u-g-e-r . . . Kruger . . . Von Kruger.
Q. So your full name is Hans Von Kruger?
A. Yes.
Q. What rank do you hold in the military?
A. Lieutenant.
Q. Are you studying then in a naval academy of some kind?
A. I have just come out of the academy.
Q. I now want you to move forward in time six months. (Instructions given.)
A. I'm going to get my ship.
Q. What will be your duties?
A. We will be protecting the coast of the Netherlands.
Q. What year is it, Hans?
A. 1812.
Q. Do you have a girlfriend?
A. Yes . . . Gretchen.
Q. When will you see her again?
A. I won't.
Q. Have you broken up with her?
A. No . . . I'm going to sea.
Q. Won't you see her when you come back?
A. I won't be back.
Q. What do you mean, you won't be back? Do you have a premonition that you won't be back?

A. Yes . . . I will never return.

Q. Do you feel this knowledge is due to a psychic ability you have?

A. I don't understand your question.

Q. All right, disregard that question. Let's move forward in time again a full year. You will be twenty-one years old. (Instructions given.)

A. I'm at sea . . . I'm ill . . . fever.

Q. (Instructions given to rise above the physical sensations.) Are there many others on board that have the fever?

A. Yes . . . we're lost.

Q. How long have you been lost?

A. Days.

Q. Let's move forward in time three months. (Instructions given.)

Further questioning established that at this time they were no longer lost but were still at sea. Many had been killed by the fever. The name of the ship was the *Dresden*. Hans felt that the captain was cruel and unjust in punishment, and he didn't like him. At twenty-three he saw himself in an English harbor, awaiting repairs incurred during a bad storm. At this time he regretted joining the navy and did not like his duties.

(End of second session)

After she was awakened, we all spent the rest of the evening discussing the regression and metaphysics in general. It was a totally new experience and way of thinking for Jane, and she didn't know quite what to make of it at all. She had no strong religious beliefs but was unready to accept reincarnation until she knew more about it.

I was curious about her background and found that she had come to Phoenix two years earlier, with her son from a first marriage, to take a job as a secretary for American Express. She had lived in Tennessee previously, and had experienced four miscarriages before having the one child, an eight-year-old named William. Jane's mother had also moved to Phoenix, and the three of them were presently sharing an apartment.

Don had moved from Wisconsin to Phoenix, was also divorced, and had a boy about the same age as William.

In the weeks that followed, Jane and Don became quite involved, and I heard that they were considering living together. I talked with Don about doing some more sessions to further the understanding of the information we had already received. They both agreed, and this time I first attempted to hypnotize Don, but without success. He was more than cooperative and desired the experience but could not ease into a trance. (It was later discovered through subsequent regression with Jane that she and Don had also been together in Egypt, and he had been part of the mystery schools. One of the teachings in such schools was to avoid hypnosis for fear of outside mind control. Actual blocking techniques were part of the curriculum.)

Jane was by now a well-conditioned subject and easily went into the deepest trance.

Jane

Third Regression Session

December 1972

We had already received considerable information about the Dutch lifetime, but we knew nothing of the karmic ties that might have resulted from the previous incarnation. I decided, instead of regressing Jane again, to take her up into the higher-self, or superconscious, all-knowing mental realms of her own mind. This technique is not always successful, but Jane was an exceptionally good subject and was easily carried to this state of expanded mental awareness. The session was long and complicated, and the transcripts could confuse the case, so it is easier to explain the knowledge that was derived from it.

> Jane was Hans in the Dutch life and was raised Catholic.
> Don was Gretchen in the Dutch life and was Jewish.
> They had wanted to marry, but Hans's mother was extremely forceful in preventing it. Hans, frustrated over the trauma of the situation and feeling it was hopeless, went to sea. Jane's mother in her present life was Hans's mother in the Dutch incarnation.
> After Hans was gone, Gretchen gave birth to his son. She awaited her lover's return and was happy with her son. Years later she received word that Hans had been killed, and from that time on she saw the child as a constant reminder of a love she could never have, and grew to dislike the child. Gretchen had been an attractive woman with a beautiful body but she let herself go, becoming fat and unkempt. Three years later she also died.
> Jane's present son had been Gretchen's son in the previous life.

Once this karmic information had been received, we spent the rest of the session experimenting. Jane became extremely psychic while in the higher-self and was able to tell me many things about myself and my past that she or Don had absolutely no way of consciously knowing. She also predicted several forthcoming events in my own life, all of which happened exactly as predicted in the weeks that followed. At the time, her son was just beginning to undergo medical tests for a physical problem, and I asked her if she could diagnose his illness. She responded with an extensive description of the problem and causes, which can be summarized as an imbalance in a particular glandular system. In the days that followed, Don gave this information to the doctor at the A.R.E.

Clinic in Phoenix (The Association of Research and Enlightenment—the Edgar Cayce Society). His medical reaction was "possible but highly unlikely; it would be one of the last things we'd check." Yet a few days later the tests confirmed the accuracy of Jane's diagnosis from the higher-self hypnotic trance.

When Jane and Don had first met, they were immediately attracted to each other, despite the fact that neither had ever been attracted to the other's type before. Don is tall and blond, and he likes tall, thin women. Jane is short and overweight and had always been turned off by large blond men.

As strongly as Don was attracted to Jane, he was equally repulsed by her son, William. Don was used to being around children and usually loves them, but he was irritated by William's every word and action, and he couldn't understand his own reactions.

Jane, living with her mother and the boy, was also developing hostile feelings toward her own son. The grandmother was becoming more and more of a problem in her domination of both Jane and the boy, and she constantly voiced her dislike of Don.

Money was a heavy burden to Don at the time, and he was using a family debt counselor to help straighten out his life in this area. Both Jane and Don tried on several occasions to pull away from each other. They both went out and became involved with others, but they were always pulled back together, through circumstances and through their own mental and physical needs.

At Christmastime that year I found a small gift-wrapped package on the seat of my car. The tag read, "Merry Christmas from Hans and Gretchen." Inside was a pair of miniature wooden shoes.

I met with Jane and Don again shortly after that. Their lives had not calmed down, but they were together and still talking about living together. We decided to do another hypnosis session, searching for enlightenment in the area of karmic interaction.

Jane

Fourth Hypnosis Session

January 1973

Hypnosis was induced and again Jane was instructed
to return to the higher-self realms of her mind. The
karmic reasons for the relationship problems were complicated and affecting all four of the people within the
present situation: Don, Jane, her son and mother. Again
it is easier to explain the information received through
the session.

William in this life was Gretchen's (Don's) son
in their last lives. He was still carrying subconscious
resentments from the past.

Don's uncommon aversion to overweight females
was due to his own subconscious dislike of himself
in this position as Gretchen. Gretchen disliked herself and became fat when she lost Hans.

Hans wasn't true to himself when he allowed his
parents to interfere with his plans to marry Gretchen.
So Jane was now being forced to experience,
through the problems with her own mother, the same
tests once again.

Hans (Jane) had walked out on his responsibility
to a child in his last life. In this life Jane had to go
through four miscarriages to finally have a child of
her own—to show that she really wanted the child.
She was also allowed to have only one child in this
life, due to a hysterectomy.

Jane's present problems with weight were a balance from the past. When Hans left Gretchen, it
hurt her mentally, resulting in the development of an

overweight condition. Jane was experiencing a karmic effect.

William, being kinetic and sickly, was becoming a mental drain to his mother. Jane will have to live up to the responsibility she had desired, before she'll be allowed more children in a future life. William is a karmic tie and test.

(End of fourth session)

A few weeks later Don and Jane rented a house and moved in together. The grandmother tried everything short of legal action to break up the situation, to the point of attempting to talk Jane's first husband into initiating such an action. This time around Jane stood up to the parental interference, but experienced constant badgering for months, through the grandmother's mental indoctrination of William. When allowed to take the child for a weekend, the grandmother would rave to him about his mother's "living in sin," and the Bible's condemnation of reincarnational thinking.

For the next several months life was not easy, but Don and Jane understood their Karma and both were dedicated to rising above it. The money problems continued. There was sickness in the family, and the problems with William were more intense than ever, but by the end of the year there was far more understanding and better interaction among all involved. Don accepted his responsibilities with the child, and through patience and considerable hard work, proved to be a stabilizing and positive influence, resulting in an obvious improvement in the relationship.

In December 1973 Don and Jane were married in a small metaphysical ceremony in their home. The psychic, Kingdon Brown, performed the ceremony, and I stood up with Don. Through working together on the regressions, and in other areas, Don and Jane became very close friends with me and remain so to this day. Don developed his own abilities with hypnotic regression, and we have often worked and experimented together.

One of the more interesting experiments is something

we call a Chalkra Linkup, and we're both still working with the idea. There are seven chalkras (energy points) in the human body, and Yoga/metaphysical thinking incorporates the development of these areas. The lower chalkras are already developed in most of us, but the higher points require physical discipline and an expanded awareness.

The linkup is achieved by having two people lying side by side, usually holding hands, while a third person induces a deep state of hypnosis. Jane and I have often been subjects, while Don has induced the trance. The hypnotist then begins to link the chalkras, by having both subjects imagine the colored light of the appropriate chalkra arching between the bodies. For instance, "You will both now imagine a deep purple colored light connecting your third eyes, emitting from the center of your forehead, arching up and over to connect with the other's forehead." This is done with all seven chalkras, and when completed it has been our experience that a psychic connection takes place. When asked to send numbers back and forth, we are always able to do so correctly. While in a trance I might think the number six, and hold out six fingers so Don would be aware of the number. Jane would then be able to speak up from her trance state and say the number six.

We have also done this with designs, pictures, and past lives, both being able to tap in on the other's impressions and images. The technique has been attempted with several combinations of people with a high degree of success. If fully developed, I believe it could be a beautiful channel for understanding between two people. A way to "walk a mile in my moccasins," so to speak. In troubled relationships it could provide deep insight into another's thinking, which could be achieved in no other way.

Over the years we have completed many additional regressions with Jane. There are four known lifetimes in which she and Don have been together, and this knowledge has helped to show them a karmic pathway to a spiritual awareness they might not have known without experiencing regression.

Today Don works as a free-lance illustrator, keeping as busy as he desires to be. Jane works in a Scottsdale art gallery. They both continue to search for new knowledge through involvement with metaphysical experimentation. As of this writing they have been married for nearly two years, and they believe they are together in the present because they have known love in the past.

Sandy and Desmond

A SINGLE REGRESSION SESSION HAS OFTEN EXPLAINED the present predicaments between two people, and the case of Desmond Williams is a perfect example. He had attended several of the public Wednesday night programs at the Hypnosis Center, then made an appointment for a private session. He worked in the camera room of the local newspaper and was unable to get off during the day, so we arranged an evening appointment.

Relaxing in the controlled environment room of the Center, he explained to me that he was searching for answers and understanding in regard to his present marital problems. He'd been married twice, and a ten-year-old daughter from his first marriage was living with him and his second wife, Sandy.

"Can you give me some background on your relationship with Sandy, and the problems you are presently experiencing?" I asked.

"My first wife and I were married about four years, and when we were divorced I was awarded custody of our daughter. But that is past and of little concern at this time. Sandy and I were married almost four years ago now, and there have been numerous problems. One is my daughter . . . she and I get along beautifully, but Sandy . . . well, it's a situation of total nonacceptance. It's pretty hard to have three people living together with one of them acting as if one of the three didn't exist. Probably the biggest problem has been my work. I've had constant overtime ever since we were married. It's worked out that every time Sandy has needed me, I haven't been there . . . I've been at work. Ironically, right after she left me a few weeks ago, all my overtime stopped and won't be necessary in the future."

"Where is she now?" I asked.

"She moved out and immediately moved in with another man," he responded. "She's still married to me, but she is living with someone else, right here in Scottsdale."

"How are you handling the situation?" I asked, aware that he was trying hard to maintain his composure in discussing circumstances that had his life in a turmoil.

"I want her back. I know it's dumb, but I don't want to get a divorce. She calls me all the time and has come over twice, but we never seem to get anywhere in our discussions. If she'd leave him and come back, I could easily handle what she's done . . . and there wouldn't be any more overtime. I think she has just gone to this guy for a refuge and doesn't care that much about him. I've seen her confused before, but nothing like this."

"Is she considering coming back?' I asked.

"We talk about it. I went to a psychic, and she told me that Sandy would return by December twenty-second."

"Whatever you do, do not live for that," I responded. "Too many psychics pick up things from their clients' own minds. Your desires could be so strong that they are being transmitted. The psychic is receiving data but may not know where it is coming from. It would be very natural to desire to have her back for Christmas, and that is what is received through standard extrasensory channels. I certainly do not mean to discourage you, but I've seen too many people build their hopes and plans for something that was never based upon reality."

"Do you know how I could pull her back to me through occult channels?" he asked.

"Yes, I do," I responded. "But you will never learn how through me. First, I don't want the karma, and even more important, you must realize that you would regret it. I can't even begin to tell you how badly the use of such knowledge would reverse upon you. If you think you are feeling turmoil now, just multiply it many times."

"But I've heard of people successfully doing it," he said.

"Have you been close enough to know the results of such actions?" I asked. "I've received many phone calls from people requesting this kind of help, but anyone who is responsibly committed to psychic work will never become involved, other than to try to discourage them. I try to talk them into mentally sending the person they're concerned about light and love. Concentrate on sending calming, positive thoughts, which will result in positive karma regardless of whether you get back together or not."

"I love her so much," he said, with tears almost coming into his eyes. "I know you're right, but, God, I want her to come back. I want a chance to make it right again."

"From my perspective, Desmond, and I know this probably doesn't help you very much right now, the effects you are experiencing are karmic. The results are probably predestined. This event was predestined, and how you handle it now is what is important now. I know it is hard to think positive at the moment, but through thinking this way you will rise above a similar situation at some time in the future."

We discussed metaphysics and interaction of karma for some time. Desmond had some knowledge but was obviously seeking understanding and enlightenment. I had observed him in trance during the Wednesday night programs and was aware that he was a deep-level hypnosis subject. I explained that we would use regressive hypnosis in an attempt to find the causes of the present-day effects. That an understanding of the past might provide insight that could help him handle the present.

Desmond

Regression Session

October 1973

Hypnosis induced and regression preparation completed. The following instructions were then given: "If you and Sandy have been together in another lifetime, I now want you to return to the past, to another time and another place. To a past life in which you have known each other. If you have been together in numerous past lives, I want your own subconscious mind to choose the lifetime that will offer the greatest understanding of your present circumstances. You will now return to a past life at the time of your first meeting with the entity who is now Sandy, if such a lifetime has transpired. If there has been no past life together, on the count of eleven you will tell me so." (Instructions given.)

Q. Speak up now and tell me what you see and what you are doing. (The subject becomes extremely emotional, and it is necessary to create an artificial environment, combined with strong calming suggestions, to relax him once again.) All right, I now want you to tell me what you are perceiving.

A. I'm in a very barren area . . . there are some white cliffs, almost desert.

Q. Is there anyone there with you?

A. No, I'm alone . . . I'm going to . . . ah . . . ah . . . a neighboring settlement . . . caves."

Q. How are you traveling?

A. I'm walking.

Q. How are you dressed? You have the ability to look down and tell me how you are dressed.

A. A loincloth.

Q. Are you male or female?

A. Male.

Q. All right, let's move forward in time until you meet with someone who is important to you. (Instructions given.)

A. I've entered a camp . . . the people live in caves and crude structures. . . . There's somebody . . . I don't know . . . somebody dark . . . I think it's a woman. . . . I'm afraid.

Q. Are you an outsider in this camp?

A. Yes . . . but I'm known to them . . . Indian.

Q. Why are you there?

A. I've come to barter for the daughter. . . .

Q. Let's move forward to the time of the actual bartering. (Instructions given.)

A. I'm sitting on the ground in front of him . . . she's sitting beside him. . . . (Emotion builds again and calming suggestions are given. Desmond is then commanded to look upon this only as an observer.)

Q. Tell me more about what is happening.

A. Her father is shaking some bones . . . and . . . oh . . . oh . . . he . . . (Emotion builds again.) The bones turned out against me . . . I'm being told to leave and never return . . . . under pain of death.

Q. All right, we're letting go of this and moving forward in time to the time you see this girl again, if indeed you ever do see her again. (Instructions given.)

A. I see what is happening. . . . It's not finished . . . I'm leaving . . . but . . . but I come back . . . it's night. . . . I take the girl . . . I take her back. I don't live in a village. . . . I live in a solitary cave and have some crops. . . . There's a stream. . . .

Q. Tell me more about what happens.

A. We're in love . . . but her father has sent men after us. . . . She is arguing with them. She won't go back with them. (Emotion builds, and subject begins to cry. Calming suggestions given.)

Q. What is the outcome of this situation? I want you to

move forward in time and explain the outcome to me. (Instructions given.)

A. She is killed. . . . I'm running away . . . oh . . .

Q. How did she die?

A. Her father . . . he clubbed her to death. (The subject is extremely emotional, so rather than continue with questioning, I move to bring the regression to a close.)

Q. I now want you to move forward in time to the last day of your life. You will not have died, but it will be the last day of your life. (Instructions given.)

A. I'm looking at the sky.

Q. How old are you now?

A. Ancient.

Q. I want you to look back over your entire life. I want you to absorb all the important information about this lifetime. Think about it and I won't question you for a few minutes. Let the understanding of your entire life now come in. You will consciously remember everything you are receiving, and when you are awakened, you will be able to discuss it with me.

Before awakening the subject, I carried him into the higher-self to find additional answers. When his wife was killed by her own father, Desmond could have stayed and fought to save her, but fled instead. The woman was pregnant with his child at the time of her death. When questioned about what had happened to him after this, he explained that he continued moving north into different terrain, and saw himself in another village. "It's completely different . . . it's woods . . . a small waterfall coming down from some cliffs . . . small village . . . sort of . . . ah . . . a long house covered with animal skins and mud. . . . Then there are some smaller ones built into the side of a hill."

An exploration of karmic ties showed that his present daughter was the soul who would have been his child in the Indian lifetime had it been allowed to be born. Sandy's father in this life was her father in the Indian

life, which Desmond felt explained the father's intense
dislike for him today.
(End of session)

It is unusual that a single session explains as much
as this one did. An obvious karmic assessment would be
that Sandy had left Desmond in this life because he had
run out on her in a prior incarnation. I'm sure she was
consciously unaware of the situation, but subconscious
hostilities were at play, creating the inner need to leave.

Two years have now passed, and there was never a
reconciliation. They were divorced several months after
this regression session. Today Desmond is actively involved with a Phoenix metaphysical group, he lives with
his brother and daughter in Mesa, Arizona, and is quite
happy with his present life.

Louise and Alex

THE MORE I RESEARCH PSYCHIC OCCURRENCES AND explore human potential, the more aware I become of the unlimited power of love. Not only is its endurance assured throughout eternity, but the love bond seems fully capable of transcending time and space, as is evidenced in the case of Alex Daniels. The name is a pseudonym, for Alex is a well-known public figure in the State of Arizona. He requested that he remain anonymous.

Our first meeting was at a Scottsdale party in 1974. Several local dignitaries and celebrities were in attendance, and during the course of the evening my work became the subject of a discussion within a small group. Alex asked if I was willing to do a private regression. We set a session date for a few days later at his home.

Sitting on the Daniels' pool patio in Paradise Valley, an exclusive community bordering Phoenix, I commented on the spectacular view. "Isn't that Senator Goldwater's home on the hill over there?" I asked.

"Right," Alex responded. "You can spot it by the huge ham radio antenna he has set up. The house didn't really fit our needs, but Louise and I were hypnotized by the view."

The lights of the city stretched out as far as we could see, broken only by the silhouette of Camelback Mountain, a local landmark.

Louise joined us on the patio, bearing a tray of snacks and drinks, and we all began to discuss the forthcoming regression. "Is there anything in particular you're interested in finding out about your past, Alex?" I inquired.

"Well, it's more a matter of curiosity than anything else. I've had some dreams that I feel might be past-life experiences, but I don't know. Of course, I'd like to know if Louise and I have been together before. She's the one that got me into all of this, and now she's afraid to experience it."

"What do you mean?"

"She started reading various psychic books about a year ago, and she'd tell me about the details and concepts. At first I teased her about being a kook, but I became intrigued and started reading Cayce's writings and several others. It seemed to ring true somehow. Anyway, when I talked with you the other night at the party, I thought that regressive hypnosis might be a way to check it out. I've been trying to talk Louise into being the subject, but she'll have no part of it."

"Even if I instruct you to re-experience only happy past-life situations?" I asked.

"Maybe some other time," she laughed. "Guess I'm afraid I might find out I was Marie Antoinette or Mata Hari!"

"What about the dream you feel might be a past-life experience?" I asked Alex.

"The reason I think it could be is that I know it's Louise in my dream, but she doesn't look like she does now. I've had it three times, and it's always a different situation, but it's the same woman. The only thing that doesn't track is that once or twice it seemed too contemporary. Once I saw her cooking on what looked like a modern-day gas range, yet the house seemed old-fashioned."

"Does it seem symbolic or disjointed?" I questioned.

"Not at all. I simply seem to be following this woman for a while as she goes about her daily activities. I've observed a child of about ten—a blond-haired boy—

with her sometimes. Once she was feeding chickens and gathering eggs. Another time there were several other women with her in a living room. Nothing very exciting."

"All right, let's see what we can find out. Where would you like to conduct the session?" The decision was made to use a tilt-back lounge chair in Alex's study. Louise wanted to observe and record the regression.

In working with hypnosis for many years, I have learned you can never be sure who will be a good subject and who won't. Too many judgments have proved incorrect, but I was concerned about Alex's ability to let go of his all-consuming reality long enough to relax and go into a deep trance. It may have been the demands of his public profession, but the outward manifestation was an analytical and hyper personality. I'd have felt easier conducting the initial session in a controlled environment with a brainwave synchronizer. As it was, I decided to incorporate all my portable equipment into the induction. The takedown can be slow and intense, but there is also the possibility of putting the subject to sleep (normal opposed to hypnotic) when this is used.

I worked slowly, carrying Alex through extensive yoga breathing, asking him to keep his eyes on the revolving hypno-disc as I worked him through the body-relaxing techniques of pre-induction. When I instructed him to close his eyes, his body muscles were obviously relaxed, so I continued to put him under. Although I seldom use tests, it seemed desirable before proceeding, if only for his own awareness—that he was in reality in a hypnotic state. "You are in a deep hypnotic sleep," I told him, "and I want you to raise your right arm. That's it, right up over your head. Your arm is now locked in that position. No matter how hard you try, you cannot lower your arm. You may try if you wish, but you will be unable to lower it. In fact, I want you to try, but your attempts will be to no avail." Alex began to strain, trying to lower his arm. The force of his attempt caused his entire body to tremble. "Stop trying . . . you may return your arm to your side."

Alex

Regression Session

December 1974

Regression preparation was completed, and the following instructions were then given: "I want you to return to a past lifetime in which you have known your present wife, Louise, if such an incarnation exists. If the dreams you have experienced are related to a prior life you've experienced together, I want you to go to that lifetime, at the time of your first meeting. If this is not the case, your own subconscious mind will choose a lifetime in which you've been together that might prove of value for you to explore at this time." (Instructions given.)

Q. I want you to speak and tell me what you are perceiving at this time.
A. She seeks work.
Q. Who seeks work?
A. The girl . . . her name is Matra. (Phonetic spelling.)
Q. What does she do?
A. She wants to learn to make pots.
Q. Why has she come to you to learn this?
A. Well . . . (Very indignant.) Who is a better potter than I?
Q. I'm sorry, I should have known. Will you give her work?
A. I'm considering it. She is quite beautiful.
Q. Did you know her before?
A. No, she claims the gods sent her to me.
Q. Do you accept that?
A. Tenia . . . (Phonetic spelling.) Maybe?
Q. Who is Tenia?

A. Our God! ! ! Who are you, anyway?

(On the tapes this sounds like Ten-yea-ah. Research showed the accepted spelling of this Etruscan deity as Tinia.)

Q. Ah . . . I'm . . . ah . . . from a faraway land and am unaware of your beliefs. I would like to learn. If the girl works for you, will you pay her?

A. I will not pay her! (Indignant again.) She will be allowed to learn, but she will never be a potter. She is a woman . . . she'll have to sleep in the back.

Q. How old are you?

A. Twenty-four summers. . . . Where are you, anyway?

Q. (The subject is given strong hypnotic suggestions to alleviate his concern about talking with someone he cannot see.) I want to know what country you live in.

A. Etruria.

(Note: The Etruscans were a civilization of people living in what is now north-central Italy. Developing from the Villanovans (1000 B.C.), they initially controlled even the city of Rome. By 290 B.C. the Etruscans, who were influential in the development of the Roman Empire, were subdued by it.)

Q. I want to know about the pots you make.

A. They are the finest.

Q. Ah, all right . . . what are they used for?

A. To observe . . . for water . . . for fire people.

Q. Fire people?

A. For the remains of those who have entered the underworld.

Q. Do you mean that upon their death they were burned, and their ashes are retained in the pots?

A. Yes.

Q. What color are your pots?

A. Black. (I felt that the subject was once more becoming disgusted with me for asking such foolish or obvious questions.)

Q. I want you now to move forward in time three months

and tell me what is happening at that time. (Instructions given.)

A. I allow her to help me.

Q. Matra?

A. Yes . . . she works the clay.

Q. What do you feel about Matra?

A. I now allow her to sleep with me.

Q. How nice of you. Is she happy with this arrangement?

A. Of course.

Q. Tell me about your position in society. Are you respected? Do you do well?

A. Of course! (Indignant again.) My work is prized in Rome.

Q. So you trade with the Romans. What can you tell me about Rome?

A. We rule them, but they are rebellious. We teach them, and now the incompetent fools attempt to duplicate my pots ! !

Q. Let's change the subject. Do you plan to marry Matra?

A. Why?

Q. All right, let's move forward in time. I want you to move forward a few days or months or years . . . until something very important transpires between you and Matra. (Instructions given.) What is happening?

A. She is with child.

Q. What do you feel about this?

A. Now I'll have to marry her.

Q. Do you love her?

A. I guess so.

Q. Then getting married won't be so bad, will it?

A. It won't change anything.

Q. I'm glad you feel so positive about it. How long has it been since she first came to ask you about work?

A. One summer.

Q. When you say one summer, do you mean a full year . . . ah . . . twelve months?

A. I don't understand.

Q. All right, I'll settle for one summer. Can you tell me the year or the time it is now?

A. The sun is mid-sky.

Q. I think we were better off talking about pots. Let's move forward in time once again to the time your baby is born, if indeed this does happen. (Instructions given.)

A. I have a son . . . he yells, oh, does he yell! He will make a good potter, he will become the finest potter in all Etruria.

Q. How is Matra doing?

A. Fine, fine, she is at the baby-woman's.

Q. Who is the baby-woman?

A. She has a place twelve houses from here. She helps with babies.

Q. Did she help to deliver your baby?

A. Of course, I just told you.

Q. Let's move forward in time once again. We are going to move forward five years. (Instructions given.) What is happening now?

A. The times are bad, there is revolt. We fight Rome.

Q. Why do you fight Rome?

A. We have always had trouble with Rome . . . though not like now. I am more concerned with the revolts here.

Q. Why is there fighting in Etruria?

A. There is fighting everywhere, it seems. It is so confusing. They would rather fight than buy pots.

Q. How is Matra and your son?

A. They are fine . . . I built another room.

Q. You mean you added another room onto your house?

A. Yes.

Q. What did you build it out of?

A. Wood and clay.

Q. Did you incorporate artistic decoration into the clay?

A. Of course. What would people think?

Q. I don't know. I have not asked your name before. Can you tell me your name?

A. Ralus.

Q. Does Matra really love you, Ralus?

A. Of course she does. She works hard for me.

Q. I had a feeling you were going to say something like

that. All right . . . let's let go of this and move forward in time once again to an important event that takes place between yourself and Matra. (Instructions given.)

A. She is hurt . . . she is hurt . . . Matra, Matra.

Q. What happened?

A. The water canal was destroyed, she walked to the other hill, to the well . . . they attacked her. I will kill them.

Q. Let's move to the next day, move forward one day and tell me what is happening now. (Instructions given.)

A. She doesn't say anything. She just sleeps. He stopped the bleeding.

Q. A doctor?

A. Yes . . . he says she will be all right. If only I knew who did this. (There is much anger in the subject's voice.)

Q. Let's move forward in time one month. (Instructions given.) How is Matra now?

A. She is working hard again.

Q. Then she has recovered?

A. Yes, but she doesn't talk as much any more.

Q. What did the men do to her?

A. They raped her and beat her. (Anger wells up in his voice again.)

Q. Did you find out who was responsible?

A. No.

Q. Does Matra make pots, or do you only allow her to work the clay?

A. She makes pots, but I sell them elsewhere.

Q. Why?

A. Because she is a woman. If they knew, they would not buy.

Q. Does she make good pots?

A. I taught her ! ! !

Q. I guess I forgot. I now want you to move forward in time once more, only this time you are going to move to the last day of your life. You will not have died or crossed over into spirit, and you will feel no pain and no emotion. (Instructions given.)

A. I'm lying on the bed . . . my head is bloody . . . can't think . . . don't seem to . . . Matra is holding my hand . . . I love you . . . I . . . (Subject stops talking.)

The subject is now instructed to move up into the higher-self realms of his own mind to answer further questions and to gain insight and understanding into his present lifetime.

Q. I want you to explain to me what happened in your lifetime as Ralus . . . how were you killed?
A. A man hit me with a club.
Q. Why did he hit you?
A. The Gauls, moving through from the north. I was in the streets and one of them hit me.
Q. How old were you at the time?
A. My son was grown.
Q. I want to ask you about something else now. The dreams you had in which you thought the woman was Louise in a past-life situation . . . what can you tell me about this?
A. (The subject is silent for a while, then speaks.) All I see is Louise standing in front of a . . . like two mirrors, one in front and one behind, and her reflection just repeats and repeats until it gets so small I can't see it any more.

(End of session)

"Oh boy!" Alex exclaimed, shaking his head as if to clear up the experience. "I feel like my mind just made up a nifty little fantasy."

"Do you consciously know anything about Etruria?" I asked.

"It doesn't even sound like a real place to me," he said, very doubting.

"Well, I'm not familiar with it either," I said. "But my knowledge of history isn't that great. I would be very much surprised, though, if you manufactured a story from the trance level you had attained."

HISTORIC FOLLOW-UP NOTES:

Etruria did exist as explained in the note during the regression. Although not as advanced as the Greeks, Etruscan towns, which included stone temples, were large and walled for defense.

The name of the major Etruscan god, Tinia, is close to the name Alex used.

Etruria was developed before Rome and controlled much of north and central Italy, including Rome, passing on many benefits of civilization to the Romans.

The Etruscans were artistic people, and pottery was an advanced art, including shiny black "bucchero" pottery.

Etruscan kings controlled Rome for about one hundred years, followed by two decades of fighting between the two powers.

Alex did the initial research work himself and called to tell me of his findings a few days after the regression session. "I don't think I made it up," he said, still sounding a little bewildered.

"Don't be so surprised, Alex. If reincarnation is a fact of life, and part of what we are all now exploring, then it is our reality. I have yet to see someone relive a lifetime within the boundaries of known history and not be able to verify at least some of the facts, if they experienced it while in a deep trance."

"I always have to know the hows and whys of everything. I read about genetic memory, but that theory doesn't seem to be valid to me. Let me ask you directly. If I was not seeing my own past life, what was I seeing? Is there any other explanation?"

"There is one other theory which I believe should be considered, but it may only confuse you more," I explained. "You are a particular energy frequency; I use the term 'energy frequency' opposed to 'soul.' That energy is exploring a potential by living a physical life on the earth. Now I have come to believe, through my own research and through many other channels, that it is quite possible for that same energy to be exploring an unlimited number of potentials at the same time. In other words, and I'm only speaking symbolically, you may now be ten other people in the world, nine discarnate identities, and also forty-seven life forms on other planets or in galactic systems. You may have been two or twenty other people at the time of the Etruscan incarnation. Now everything that happens to all the identities who are part of the same energy frequency affects them all. You are all one, so you all intuitively feel the effects of the whole. This concept does not negate any existing aspect of metaphysical thought, it simply expands it. In regression I believe you could return to any of the lifetimes that were explored by your energy frequency in the past. In other words, I might find you in several lifetimes in 1621. Each would be valid and might carry obvious ties that affect your present life. One would probably be the direct extension of your individual identity, and the one we would most likely tap into in regression, unless otherwise instructed."

"I almost wish I hadn't asked," Alex said, sounding more bewildered than ever.

Several weeks later I heard from Alex and Louise Daniels again. Louise was anxious to experience her own past and wondered if I would be willing to regress her the next time I was in Phoenix.

Louise

Regression Session

January 1975

Louise was a good hypnotic subject, although her trance depth did not equal Alex's. Regression preparation was completed, and the following instructions were then given:

"I now want you to return to a past lifetime in which you have known your present husband, Alex, if indeed such a lifetime has transpired. On the count of eleven it will be at the time of your first meeting."

Q. What do you see and what are you doing at this time?
A. I'm washing up . . . been plowing all day.
Q. Are you male or female?
A. Male.
Q. Tell me what else is happening.
A. I'm just going inside.
Q. Into your home?
A. My parents' home . . . we have some new neighbors, and they've come to call.
Q. Are they there now?
A. Yes . . . my mother and father and the new people. They have their daughter with them.
Q. How old is the daughter?
A. My age . . . ah . . . maybe a little younger. . . . Their farm is down the road from ours.
Q. How old are you?
A. Nineteen.
Q. What country are you living in now?
A. France.
Q. What year is it?
A. 1846.
Q. Tell me what the conversation is about.
A. They're just talking about crops and that sort of thing. . . . She sure is pretty.
Q. Are you talking with the daughter?
A. No, we just keep kind of looking at each other. I think she's embarrassed.
Q. All right, if you have further contact with this girl, I now want you to move forward in time, to that time. (Instructions given.)
A. I'm in the fields, she is bringing me something . . . a drink.
Q. Tell me more about what is happening.
A. She's . . . ah . . . well, she has a copper pot of tea. Like we make from dried mint. . . . It's . . . ah . . .

cold. She is really pretty and laughing. She said she got her clean dress all dirty in the field. My father is yelling at me to get to work.

Q. I want to ask you a few questions. What is your name, and her name?

A. My name is Victor. Hers is Marie.

Q. Who rules France at this time?

A. Philippe . . . but from what I've heard it may not be for long.

Q. Why not?

A. There is a reform movement. . . . I don't understand much of it. I can only read a little, and they say you can't trust what is printed anyway.

Q. How far away is Paris?

A. Five days.

Q. Let's move forward in time again. You will move forward two years. (Instructions given.) What is happening now?

A. I'm playing with the baby.

Q. Is this your baby?

A. Marie's and mine.

Q. Then you were married?

A. Yes, thirteen months ago.

Q. Where are you living now?

A. We have a small place. My father helped me build it on the southeast corner of his land.

Q. You're still helping your father to farm then?

A. Uh-huh. (Subject seems distant, as if occupied elsewhere.)

Q. Are you and Marie happy?

A. Very happy. . . . I wish she wouldn't tell me what to do so often, but I love her.

Q. How does Marie spend her day?

A. Sewing, cooking . . . taking care of the boy.

Q. Do you have any hobbies or things you like to do when you have free time?

A. There is little free time . . . but I like to make things. During the winter I worked a piece of metal from an old wagon into a knife. Then I carved a handle out of a piece of bone . . . and carved a picture into it.

Q. What kind of picture?

A. Oh, just lines curving around and shapes.

Q. How is the political situation in France at this time?

A. Philippe fled to England . . . at least that's what I heard.

Q. What else have you heard?

A. Not much . . . it all sounds very confusing. Many people in the cities are not working, and there is trouble. They should farm the land . . . then they wouldn't have time to worry about other things.

Q. Let's move forward in time again until something important happens. (Instructions given.)

A. My father died. (The subject becomes emotional and is given instructions to experience this only as an observer.)

Q. How did this happen?

A. He was working in the fields and he just fell over. It's a day's ride to the doctor . . . and . . . and when I got back he was already dead.

Q. Let's move forward again until another important event takes place. (Instructions given.)

A. I'm sick . . . so hot . . . oh . . . can't seem to . . . seem to . . .

Q. (Subject is given instructions not to feel the physical sensations.) Speak up and explain to me what has happened.

A. Have trouble breathing . . . have been working almost night and day . . . trying to farm it by myself, but I can't . . . I can't. . . . (Sobs.)

A series of questions and answers at this point established that Victor had pneumonia. Since his father's death he had taken over the entire workload of the farm. It was now late fall of 1859. In asking about his relationship with Marie, he explained, "We fight a lot, but we always get over it." At this time they had three children, two boys and a girl. Victor's mother had passed away, but Marie's parents were still living nearby and her mother was there helping to care for Victor.

Q. I now want you to move to the last day of your life. You will not have died, but it will be the last day of your life. (Instructions given.)

A. Have to get up . . . have to . . . back to . . . there is so much to . . .

Q. What are you doing now?

A. Getting up . . . my chest hurts when I pull on my boots. . . . So hot . . . don't need my coat.

Q. Where is Marie?

A. Sleeping . . . she's been up so much with me . . . sleeping.

Q. Tell me exactly what you're doing now.

A. Walking to the barn . . . so much snow, but it's not cold. . . . Oh . . . ah . . . oh . . .

Q. Tell me.

A. I fell down . . . dizzy . . . sleepy . . . oh . . . Marie . . . Marie ! !

(End of session)

"No wonder I hate snow so much," Louise said upon being awakened from the trance. "I begged my parents to let me come to Arizona to attend ASU. I grew up in Northern Michigan, and since childhood I sought to escape winter."

"I can't even talk her into going to Flagstaff to ski," Alex interrupted, laughing.

"Not much else seems to tie in," she said. "If there is anything I'm not interested in, though, it is this 'back to the land' movement. Farming has always sounded like a living hell to me. One thing I forgot to tell you after you regressed Alex—I'd taken pottery while in college and was very good at it."

"Well, Marie," I said, addressing Alex, "how are you doing with the sewing and cooking this time around?"

"Enough of that . . . ever since I met you my head's been working overtime on things that I've never had to consider before. Do you have any idea the amount of reassessment this philosophy, or whatever it is, creates?"

"Yes, but for my own curiosity, give me some examples."

"Church, for one thing. I'm not much of a Christian by the church's standards, I suppose, but we do attend the Presbyterian church, and I'm on a couple of committees. How does all this fit in?"

"We're talking about a belief system based upon love, freedom, and justice. Metaphysical thinking transcends organized religion and explains it, without negating your existing concepts—except for those based on fear. Admittedly, as within any belief system, there is some dogma, but it is a dogma of self in relationship to the whole. I believe there is a much larger reality that transcends metaphysics, but for now, or until we can free our concepts, it is the outer framework of the belief system of the entire energy gestalt, or world as we perceive it."

This statement created a discussion that lasted for the next couple of hours. "I guess one of the reasons I tend to accept it all," Alex said, "is because to live your life by this philosophy you would be a better person, by my way of thinking. There is no way to lay your responsibility upon someone else. In fact if the whole world believed it and acted accordingly, it would be a much better place to live. I'm glad you're not an advocate of hedonism," he said, looking at me. "You'd be too damn convincing in explaining it to people."

The historical facts in Louise's regression were all verified, but I did not talk with Alex and Louise again for several months. It was in late August 1975, after working with a couple of fine channel mediums, that I recalled Alex's dreams about Louise. I had an idea now of what they actually amounted to but did not want to disclose it to Alex before checking it out. I called him the first week of September.

"Alex, I'm doing some psychic research with a woman in Phoenix, and I wonder if you'd be willing to go over to her house for an hour or so next week to check out some theories of mine."

"Sure, but what's it all about?"

"Do you know what a channel medium is?"

"I have an idea," he responded. "Someone who can let dead people talk through them?"

"Yes, I don't believe I think of 'dead' quite the way you do, but this woman has channeled considerable information to me, which has proved to be extremely accurate. I would like one of the discarnate identities who speaks through her to attempt to clarify the dreams you had about Louise looking like someone else."

The next Friday afternoon Alex and I arrived at the modest apartment of the sixty-five-year-old woman, named Ruth, I had discussed with him. She does not do public readings and is not involved with the psychic movement in Phoenix, preferring to live a quiet "Christian life," as she puts it. Ruth developed the channel ability in her mid-thirties but seldom has discussed it outside her own family. Living alone and in good health, with two birds and a cat, she seems quite happy and content with her present situation.

We sat in her living room and talked of the subject about which we were seeking knowledge. She rocked slowly in an old rocking chair, seeming to drift away . . . then another, seemingly much younger voice said, "Hello again, Richard."

"Hello, Kalla," I answered, then went on to explain the situation and asked if she could help us.

"Close your eyes," she said, speaking to Alex. "Visualize your wife in every detail so I can achieve a union with her vibrational frequency."

Alex closed his eyes and concentrated on Louise for several minutes.

"Oh, yes." Kalla finally spoke. "You may not comprehend this in its entirety but she is now here with me. She is also picking up your little girl at her school. They plan to go shopping together . . . but she is also in Iowa preparing dinner for several guests who will soon be arriving."

I looked at Alex; his mouth had dropped open, and he sat stiff on the couch, staring, transfixed, at Ruth.

Kalla continued. "The woman you saw in your dreams is your wife Louise, but she is also a woman presently living on a small farm in central Iowa. Her name is Mary and she is about thirty years of age. They are one, but separate; they are more than just these, and they know of all that they are. This is not consciously recognized, but it could be, for they are aware in the depths of their minds. There is union in sleep, and often the thoughts of one are known in the mind of the other, but it is considered their own. Mary has not always been a farmer's wife. She, her husband and son made the decision to leave the city and invest their savings in a farm about five years ago. Their place is old, but they are working hard to remodel it. The farm life is not all that they expected it to be, but they will continue to experience and learn within this environment. Prior incarnations, as you think of them, have prepared the way for further exploration of a rural life. Much that they will experience will be easy for them, for they have already solved such problems in other realities. Of course new learning will also be presented. The identity you know as Louise has chosen a different and, I might add, less familiar potential to explore within this incarnation. She is presently torn between a simple, nonmaterialistic life and the one she is now living. This is understandable but should not concern her, for we must all explore all that is. Have I answered your question?"

Alex and I climbed into my pickup and pulled out into the rush-hour traffic. "Why did I ever have to meet you?" he said, staring straight ahead without seeing the road.

I couldn't help laughing. "Look, let go of it . . . it *is,* that's all. You are becoming more fully aware of your reality. It really doesn't change your life . . . at least it doesn't detract from it in any way."

"Shit!" was his profound response. "That's easy for you to say—you've been involved with all this for half your life. But it's new to me. I have to try to fit it together. I can't talk about it with anyone but Louise, or they'll put me away."

"Want to stop for a drink?"

"Please!"

We sat in the Quilted Bear, a Scottsdale bar/restaurant, discussing the events of the afternoon. Alex excused himself to make a phone call. Upon returning to the table, he said, "Louise picked up Susan after school and they've been down at Los Arcos shopping for school clothes."

"I've got to get back to Groom Creek, we work with a psychic group every Friday night in Prescott," I told him.

" 'Oh, no, you don't," he retorted intensely. "Before you head back to your little mountain hideaway, you are going home with me to explain this afternoon to Louise, because I'm not capable of answering all the questions she's going to throw at me. I went with you, now you're coming with me."

Lynda and David

DAVID PALADIN IS CONSIDERED ONE OF THE FOREMOST Indian artists in the world today. A Navajo/Anglo who signs his work with his tribal name, "Chethlahe," he has paintings hanging in galleries and major collections throughout the world. Paladin's canvases have been auctioned for as much as eighteen thousand dollars in Europe, and the demand for his work exceeds his ability to produce.

A phenomenon and obvious success in the art world, David has been the subject of numerous national magazine articles. His achievement would enable him to live anywhere in the world, but he and his wife Lynda have chosen the small mountain town of Prescott, Arizona. Here he maintains a separate house as a painting studio and instructs a small group of young student artists. The location also allows involvement with his second love, parapsychology. As an instructor in this subject, at the free-thinking Prescott College, he directs an eager audience in metaphysical exploration and enlightenment.

I first met David shortly after moving to the mountains above Prescott, Some of his parapsychology students attended a series of group regressions I was doing with the college yoga classes. David sent word that he would like to talk with me about my work, and I dropped into his studio a few days later.

He is a bold, direct man, with a keen sense of humor

and an instantly likable personality. His appearance is more Anglo than Indian. We shook hands across a huge painting table covered with several partially finished sand paintings. David offered me some cheese and rye bread and continued to work, eat, and talk at the same time. Our conversation was a matter of feeling each other out, rapidly scanning the subject of metaphysics to find out where the other was coming from. I enjoyed it, and I know he did too. Once the foundations were established on that subject, our conversation moved into painting. He maintains a unique sense of worldly detachment toward his paintings, at the same time that he is totally immersed in the creativity and challenge.

An evening spent with the Paladins in their hilltop home proved to be one of the most interesting and enlightening I have ever experienced.

David and Lynda share a most unusual life, by anyone's standards. As we discussed psychic situations, I was overwhelmed by their involvement and the daily occurrences within their home. "We live with spooks," Lynda stated matter-of-factly. David is a psychic channel, with a number of identities speaking through him on a somewhat regular basis. Lynda converses with them all, and often receives valuable information on everything from finances to Universal understanding. David openly allows this, as long as no one is harmed in any way through the contacts. He is usually unaware of another entity speaking through him, but there is sometimes a bleed through, or different degrees of conscious perception as to what has transpired during the verbal communications.

'I'd like to clarify 'spooks,' " David injected. "Please understand this is a term of endearment. They're not fond of the word 'spirit,' and since they have a sense of humor on the other side, 'spooks' is the term we've all come to use. We don't feel that we are necessarily in contact with entities of a spiritual hierarchy—we are simply all part of the whole, experiencing life in different forms of existence for now, but there is equal dignity. They are exploring their potentials of existence on the spiritual planes, just as we are in the manifest world."

"Can you give me some examples of how you have benefited from the contacts?" I asked.

They both laughed. "Where do we even begin to start?" David said, looking at his wife. "Are you familiar with the Russian artist, Wassily Kandinsky? He died in 1944. Well, people have always compared my work to his. I started receiving information from him, subconsciously, years ago, but did not recognize the source. I was in my teens when he died, so it is not a matter of reincarnation. You might call it separate selves, but I think of it more as our being part of the same energy frequency, both on exploration of that potential. Like a limb on the tree of life, we are both leaves on one branch.

"Kandinsky, or 'Kandi,' as we call him, comes through David all the time," Lynda stated. "In fact he just solved an unusual problem for us."

"Would you mind explaining it to me?" I asked.

"I'm uninsurable," David explained, "because I had a heart attack three years ago. When it happened again recently, I really became concerned about more adequate protection for Lynda and the six children. We asked Kandi for help, and he sought out a man who had just died—metamorphized, as he calls it. Anyway, the man he found on the spiritual plane was a corporate specialist in life. He explained a complicated corporate maneuver that was little known but totally legal. I really questioned it but, upon checking with my attorney, found it to be perfect for our needs."

"Has Kandi, being an artist himself, ever helped you in your art?" I questioned, my interest peaking by this time.

"Sometimes. I had expressed in every painting medium but oil. Kandi worked in oil, so when I decided to give it a try, he worked right with me and through me. The first attempt was beautiful."

We continued to discuss the channel contacts and benefits at great length. Many were literally amazing, and often, judging from the manifested results, were beyond questioning.

"I've heard, through others, about the beautiful relationship that you and Lynda share," I mentioned. "Also some of the unusual aspects of how you got together. Would you mind explaining it to me?"

They both laughed again, sharing knowing looks and wondering where to start.

"I've heard about the photograph. Tell me about that one first if you will," I said.

"There is nineteen years' difference in our ages," David said. "I used to run away from the Indian school I attended in Santa Fe, and every time I headed to California —the Alhambra area. I don't know why, but I knew I was searching for something." (Unknown to David, Lynda was living there at the time.) "Anyway, one day I was on a cruise ship which was about to leave for Hawaii. I wasn't taking the cruise but was there saying good-bye to friends. While on board I was particularly attracted to this little girl on the deck and took a picture of her. At the time and for years after that, I could not have explained it, but you know, I carried that picture in my wallet all the way through the war. I even made up stories, telling the other guys she was my daughter. It was only after Lynda and I were married six years ago that she found the photograph and recognized that it was her. The ship identification was in the background, and she was on board saying good-bye to her grandparents, who were going to Hawaii.

"How did the two of you eventually find each other?" was the next obvious question.

"I was in my studio in Sedona and Lynda walked in to talk about my paintings. She was there on vacation from California with her mother. I was married at the time and experiencing marital problems beyond anything most people would be capable of comprehending. We had six kids, and for their sake as well as mine I had to cut the tie. The children remained with me. But back to Lynda —I only saw her that one day, but I knew. I told her I'd like to have her come visit me if she could. That was all there was to it, yet from that time on I informed everyone that she would be coming out in a year . . .

that when she got there everything would be solved. A year later she returned, and we've been together ever since."

"Did you correspond during that time?"

"One letter," Lynda interrupted, laughing.

It seemed to me that if ever two people were born again to be together, it was Lynda and David. From what I know of their relationship and the circumstances, and from what I have seen, they share a karmic bond and etheric love beyond any I have personally observed.

We discussed doing a hypnotic regression, and David was most agreeable. His own background in meditation enabled him to relax quickly and easily. I soon found I was working with a somnambulistic subject, capable of the deepest hypnotic level.

David Paladin

Regression Session

August 1975

Hypnotic trance induced and regression preparation completed. I then gave him the following instructions: "I want you to return to a past lifetime, if one exists, in which you and Lynda have been together. If you have been together in more than one lifetime, I want your own subconscious mind to choose an important and meaningful incarnation in which you have known each other." (Instructions given.)

Q. Can you speak up and tell me if you are outside or inside?

A. It's a nice garden . . . do you like my music? (David's voice is deep with a slight southwestern drawl, but the voice that answered me was much higher, speaking English, but with a heavy European accent.)

Q. Tell me about your music.

A. Ah . . . some people like it, some people don't like it . . . they say I'm too . . . hah . . . too fluttery . . . too much of a romantic . . . too much of a rebel.

Q. Is there anyone there with you at this time?

A. Ah . . . she is very beautiful . . . young . . . she likes my music . . .

Q. Can you tell me where you are—what city?

A. Munich.

Q. You're in a beautiful garden . . . is this a public place?

A. Of course . . . of course by the music room . . . oh, concerts . . . tiring sometimes . . . nothing . . . no one listens . . . oh, well."

Q. But she likes it, she likes your music?

A. Ah . . . yah . . . yah . . . (The subject drifts off into another language, almost talking to himself.)

Q. Can you tell me about your music, the type of music you play, the instruments?

A. I play the piano, I play the viola . . . mostly write . . . the harpsichord . . . but mostly piano. . . . I like Baroque music . . . ah . . . ah, it is not for this time . . . ah . . . this piece I'm writing . . . ah . . . but they will listen.

Q. Do you know the girl who is there with you, or have you just met her?

A. Ah . . . I've seen her . . . three concerts I've seen her . . . sitting, and such a beautiful face . . . ah . . . ah.

Q. What are you discussing with her?

A. She's so shy . . . but she takes my hand . . . and says . . . have courage . . . have courage . . . have courage . . . have courage. . . . People will love your music . . . but . . . the love must come within one's self first.

Q. How long have you been a musician?

A. Twelve years old . . . playing, playing, playing . . . writing, writing, playing, playing, playing, . . . writing . . . ah, but so much beauty . . . so much to explore . . . the sounds."

Q. Since you have seen this lady at the concerts, I take it that you do perform music?

A. Hah . . . they won't let me play in the symphonies? . . . I have little recitals . . . ha, ha . . . ha . . . sometimes people walk out . . . walk out, out, out . . . lots of times they sit and snore . . . or they sniffle . . . or . . . ha, ha . . . oh, people, people . . . people. . . . Why can't they listen? Just to feel. (The subject is very animated; I had someone else hand-holding the tape recorder microphone, and she had to duck as he threw his hands around in the air.)

Q. Do you feel that your music is that ahead of its time, or is that unusual?

A. Hah . . . they say I'm like Strauss . . . crazy . . . ha. . . . My music is too exciting.

Q What do you plan to do?

A. I'm writing, writing . . . beautiful story . . . folklore. . . . It's a great idea . . . a nice concept to work with. . . . I like it, I like it . . . I can make the music.

Q. Do you make enough money doing this to live?

A. What is money . . . I do not know enough of it.

Q. But you survive through your music—is that correct?

A. Ah, I have my flat, I have my flowers, my piano, I have my viola . . . and what else? . . . Sometimes a cello from a friend . . . and a house. . . . I can play . . . who needs more, except her face?

Q. Can you tell me the year it is now?

A. 1823 . . . ah . . . hum . . . hum . . . I should sing to her, but my voice is not for singing.

Q. How old are you at this time?

A. I don't think of my age . . . oh . . .

Q. All right, if something important takes place with you and the woman there with you, I now want to move forward to that time. (Instructions given.)

A. (David is smiling and chuckling to himself.) . . . ah, they like my music . . . (Laughing.) She told me the truth. . . . (Sniffles as if re-experiencing tears of joy.) I wrote it for you. (He was obviously talking directly to the woman.)

Q. Tell me about your relationship with this lady at this time.

A. She's my mother . . . she's my wife . . . she's my lover . . . she's my friend. . . . She's so patient . . . gives up so much . . . but for her . . . ah . . . and they like it. (Sniffles again.)

Q. How much time has transpired since you first met her?

A. There's no time . . . seems like forever. . . . (Starts talking low, to himself again.)

Q. But you feel through her help you won public acceptance?

A. Acceptance is nothing . . . it is for her. . . . I wanted some joy. . . . She works so hard . . . making the lace.

Q. Is making lace her profession, then?

A. She helps . . . helps to feed us.

Q. Were you married?

A. Ah, yah, yah. (Laughs.)

Q. How long have you been married?

A. Five years.

Q. Are there any children?

A. Nah, nah . . . there's no children . . . who needs . . . we have each other.

Q. Where are you performing now?

A. I am not performing, they don't let me perform . . . ha . . . ha, ha, ha, I'm not a good enough musician, but I can sit and listen . . . ah.

Q. Can you tell me your name?

A. Adolphe Adam . . . I have told you many times. (David seems very indignant that I did not know his name.)

Q. O.K. . . . ah . . .

A. (He breaks in.) Someday they will know, someday the name . . . they will know.

Q. What is your primary goal? Do you want the people to accept your music?

A. I want people to be happy . . . to learn the joy of feeling . . . feeling what one creates . . . what one has in one's heart . . . to share it.

Q. Are you involved in any other creative endeavors aside from music?

A. Ah . . . my flowers . . . ha . . . they think I'm crazy.

Q. Do you still live in the same flat?

A. Where else? . . . It is comfortable.

Q. And your wife goes to work daily?

A. No . . . she works in the house.

Q. She works in the house, helping to make the lace?

A. Sometimes her fingers . . . they bleed. . . . Poor Schatzy . . . (David lapses into a foreign language.)

Q. All right, I'd like to move forward in time one year now. (Instructions given.)

A. Write, write, write . . . music, music, music . . . ah, it's better, better than before. . . . Schatzy, ah . . .

Q. You're doing better financially?

A. Yah . . . we get paid . . . finally, finally.

Q. Can you speak to me for a moment in German? (This is actually undesirable to attempt in a regression. The subject is communicating the concepts he is re-experiencing and usually does not realize he isn't speaking in the language native to him at the time. This question often tends to confuse and can pull the present conscious mind back into the past. Experiments have shown that although the subject is speaking in English, the language of the present life, he is usually able to understand fully the language of the past life, if there is someone who can speak it with him. There was no one present who could speak either French or German, but because David was an exceptional subject, I decided to attempt to have him speak to me in the language of Adolphe Adam.)

A. (David speaks a couple of sentences to me in German.) . . . that's good. . . . (More German.)

Q. What have you said to me? I don't understand German, so you will have to explain.

A. Ah . . . ha . . . I speak to you just to say what I said . . . it is better . . . I think it is better she does not have to work so hard.

Q. What has happened in your life in the last year that has made things easier for you?

A. They perform my music . . . and . . . now I get other

commissions to write more. . . . They want another ballet . . . ah.

Q. Is this not very satisfying to you?

A. Ah . . . it matters not . . . but if it brings joy . . . and that's good.

Q. What do the respected music critics have to say about your music?

A. (He speaks a German word in disgust.) ah . . . some . . . ah . . . what do they know? They make up words . . . they don't even know what . . . ah . . . words, words, words . . . they don't understand music . . . they play at being intellectuals. (He is almost yelling, throwing his arms around. The girl holding the microphone has to move out of the way.) Always playing.

Q. Are you still living in the same city?

A. No . . . no. . . . (He says a word that is hard to hear on tape, but that sounds something like "Eastbroughten.") It's nice . . . oh, we have a garden now, she likes to see . . . oh, Schatzy.

Q. Do you take care of the garden yourself?

A. Nobody else.

Q. What about your wife? Is Schatzy interested in the flowers and the garden?

A. Ah, yah . . . yah . . . she likes except for the bugs.

Q. When you are writing your music what instruments do you compose for?

A. Piano first . . . ah . . . viola, cello . . . and my friends they orchestrate . . . and they *devastate! ! !* (David yells the words and tosses his hands in the air in mock frustration.) Ha . . . ha . . . ha . . . ah . . . ah, they can't transpose . . . they keep putting in da-da-da-da-DA . . when it should go da-da-da-da-da . . . ah . . . de, dum dum. (Begins to speak in German again.)

Q. All right, I want you now to move forward in time to the last day of your life. You will not have . . . (Rather than listening to the complete instructions, he immediately moves to the death experience, grabs his heart, and experiences death as Adolphe Adam.)

A. Ah . . . yah . . . that hurt. . . . She fights . . . her hands are cool . . . oh . . . so cool.

Q. Can you communicate to me what happened?

A. I had to leave. . . . I had to leave poor Schatzy. . . . (Lapses into German.)

Q. Why did you have to leave her?

A. Oh . . . oh . . . drifting . . . oh . . . (The subject is confused at this time. When asked what his wife's name is, he is slow to answer. Then in David's normal voice he calls out, "Lynda . . . Lynda . . ." The German voice then comes in.) Schatzy . . . Freda . . . ah . . . all over, where are you? . . . She's all over . . . each one is . . . ah . . . sleep . . . dreams . . . there's no body, only dreams . . . ah.

Q. Have you left your body?

A. Yah . . . where do I want to go? . . . Have to finish work . . . where . . . where can I finish my work?

Q. Describe the environment you find yourself in at this time.

A. Music . . . fire . . . light . . . everything's exploding beautifully . . . everything's one.

Q. Is there anyone else there with you at this time? Can you feel the presence of anyone else?

A. Ah . . . yah . . . everything is with me . . . ha . . . everything is with me . . . I am everything.

David was now instructed to let go of what he was experiencing and move up into the higher-self, all-knowing level of his own mind. (Instructions given.)

A. Yellow . . . gold . . . such a beautiful yellow. (David is answering in his own voice.)

Q. All right, I want you to absorb the beautiful, calming vibrations you find at this level of your own mind. (Subject was given time to relax and absorb knowledge.) I now want you to speak up and tell me what happened at the end of your life as Adolphe Adam.

A. My heart . . . such pain for a moment . . . and then such joy.

Q. Was Schatzy there with you at the time of death?

A. She is always with me.

Q. All right, from the perspective you have now attained,

you have an understanding of the relationship ties with the woman, Lynda, who is now your wife and was your wife Schatzy in Germany. Can you tell me if there have been other lifetimes in which the two of you have been together?

A. Ha . . . how many stars are there in the sky? How many drops of rain?

Q. Tell me of some of the other lifetimes in which the two of you have been together.

A. San Francisco . . . I'm dying . . . but she's there . . . friend . . . washing my face, giving me food . . . my face is gone . . . ah . . huh . . . no. . . . What's happened? . . . I'm all blown up . . . blown up.

Q. Can you tell me another lifetime in which the two of you have been together?

A. It's a never-ending song . . . we must be together . . . we must help . . . we must work . . . it's beautiful, our island . . . so beautiful, the sea, the peacefulness . . . and yet we know they are coming . . . those Greeks . . . with their spears . . . the end is near.

The regression was carried through two more past lives in which David and Lynda have been together. Considering the material we were receiving, I'd have loved to have questioned him all night, but it was advisable to return him to the present.

(End of session)

I had not given David a suggestion to remember everything he had experienced during the regression, and being a somnambulist subject, he awakened feeling as if he had taken a nice nap, recalling nothing that had transpired.

There were eight others present during the session, and as it ended I became aware of the intense vibrations in the room. Four of the observers were witnessing regression for the first time and were sitting, staring transfixed, at David—in a minor state of shock.

"You're one hell of a subject," I told him as a monumental understatement.

Lynda served coffee, and we all discussed the session,

playing the tape recording and theorizing about its contents. David was amazed at the change in his own voice and the facts we had discovered. "I love the ballet *Giselle*," he said. "We have the phonograph record."

Lynda explained that she too loved it, and said she had once observed David seem to drift into a trance while it was playing, moving his hands as if conducting an orchestra. Conducting music he had written for her, more than a hundred years before they met again in this lifetime.

David had no conscious knowledge of Adolphe Adam, other than his affinity for this particular ballet. "I don't know what else he did, I haven't seen any other records of his works on the market," he said.

HISTORIC FOLLOW-UP NOTES:

Adolphe Adam (1803-1856) was a little-known French composer who created thirty-nine operas and fourteen ballets during his life. *Giselle* was his most famous ballet and seems to be the only one to have stood the test of time.

Adolphe's father was a musician and forbade his son to become involved in musical activities. The boy respected his father's wishes until about the age of twelve, when he began to practice secretly. His father eventually relented and allowed Adolphe to enter the Conservatoire in 1817.

Adolphe Adam did spend time in Germany, writing ballets which were eventually performed in Berlin.

He died very suddenly, although research was unable to uncover the exact cause.

In the weeks that followed, David and I worked closely in psychic research. He receives automatic writing in the same way he becomes a channel, unaware of what is received until he reads it later. This technique has resulted in literally volumes of material which Lynda has typed and filed away. Until now it had been only for the Paladins' personal enlightenment.

"I've been receiving the stuff for years," he said. "Some-

times I'm asking a question about a particular subject,
sometimes it just flows in, unsolicited, so to speak. Much
of it has been verified in indisputable ways. If you care
to believe it, some of the material is coming from other
galaxies out in space."

One afternoon in his studio, while going over some of
this writing, David was telling me about another lifetime
in which he and Lynda had been together. "We were a
priest and a nun in Europe," he said. "Of course I don't
believe we were actually these identities. I wasn't actually
Adolphe Adam either, for that matter."

"Huh?" was my stunned reply.

"No, Adolphe Adam was Adolphe Adam. He was
never anyone else and will never be anyone else. He is
discarnate as you perceive it, but he will never be dead;
he is simply exploring his potentials in a different reality
from our own. There is no such thing as death. I am
David Paladin, and I will always be David Paladin. I
carry all the memories of Adam, because I am an exploration of his potential."

"I'm afraid I'm not grasping all that," I replied.

"You think of reincarnation as one soul being reborn
into incarnation after incarnation, in parallel time as you
comprehend it."

"Yes."

"Well, I see it a bit differently. What I believe does not
negate reincarnation, but it looks at it from a different
perspective and expands the concept considerably. As a
way of explaining it simply and almost symbolically, look
at it like this: When Adolphe Adam metamorphized
(died) he transcended to a nonphysical reality. His
knowledge and energy remain throughout eternity as
Adolphe Adam, but he was now free to explore new
potentials. Thoughts are energy and they create, they are
creating your life right now, and they will create your
future. In nonphysical existence the energy of thought
can be manifested as directed reality. Let's say Adam decided he would like to explore several new potentials—as
an example, a physical life as society woman in England,
and as a pigmy in South America, and as a Navajo/Anglo

artist in Arizona. Thus he created us as extensions of himself, as explorations of potential. Once anything is created, it is free, so the three of us are now individual identities with our own free will, but Adam can 'feel' and experience this exploration through us. In that we are all on the same frequency, so to speak, we intuitively receive information from one another, and through, for lack of better words, a system of 'spiritual genetics,' we share a knowledge of a past-life lineage. If you regressed the woman in England, she too might go back to a lifetime as Adolphe Adam."

"Can you carry it out a little further, David?"

"Well, I've explained it very simplistically. In my own case there may have been others between Adam and myself, but the lineage exists. If you carry it all the way out, it illustrates how, in reality, we are all part of the whole. We are all God. We all have the power to create individually, but at the same time we are all part of the same gestalt, or whole."

"All right, I think I'm starting to grasp it," I said. "As another example, using myself: Someone on the other side, let's say a Mayan Indian named Popul, decided he wanted to explore the potential of a white American, with artistic ability and psychic interests. So he created me as an identity to explore this potential. Although I am consciously unaware of it, he is feeling what I feel, experiencing what I am experiencing. My intuitive abilities might be carry-overs from his own. When I experience regression to a lifetime as Popul, I am actually experiencing the lifetime of my creator?"

"Your creator, or one of his lineage," David responded. "But remember, you are free to act with your own free will. God created you. Popul is God, you are God, we are all God."

"Would some of my ideas and influences actually be coming from maybe several other identities that Popul created? Let's say he also created a Swedish musician. Would some of my own musical concepts or abilities be intuitively received from this musician now living in Sweden?"

"Certainly."

"O.K., then you believe that when you die, as we think of it, you will go on to do your own creating of potentials . . . physical lives? That I will do the same thing?"

"Yes, you are Dick Sutphen, you have never been anything but Dick Sutphen, and you will always be Dick Sutphen. You are energy and you will continue to expand and explore new potentials of that energy."

"Do you feel that you might explore other potentials than physical life on the earth plane?"

"Of course, there are billions of potentials," David responded. "Life on the earth plane is a basic belief system, which, while exploring, we operate within, yet in reality we are not limited to it. We can expand the boundaries. That's what psychics do—they expand their belief system to encompass a larger reality, even though most of them still limit their potential. They could carry their abilities much further if they only believed they could. We are all unlimited in what we can do, if we open ourselves to a limitless belief."

"All right, David, Kandi often talks to me through you, from the nonphysical reality he is presently exploring. I can see that I've been understanding him on one level, when he is actually talking from a much different level. Is Kandi actually exploring physical life on the earth at this time? Has he created his own potentials which he can presently 'feel' and experience?"

"Ha, ha! . . . You finally begin to see the picture." The heavy Russian-accented voice that answered me was by now familiar, that of Wassily Kandinsky, the world-famous artist. "To answer your question, I am a woman in China at this time, and a soldier in North Vietnam, and many, many others.'

"Does the woman in China, as an example, Kandi, have any involvement with art at this time? Has she carried intuitive artistic knowledge from you?"

Kandi laughs. "No, she could if she desired to use it, but she is a good whore."

"Is she aware of you, and the others now living who are also explorations of your potential?"

"Intuitively, but not consciously. She could be, if she opened and freed herself of her limited belief system . . . as could you. You are in the process of achieving this, and you will."

"If I'm only one identity of a joint exploration, can you give me an example of another person who is also part of that exploration, someone else who is on my own frequency, so to speak?"

"Are you familiar with the Swiss sculptor and painter Alberto Giacometti?"

"No, I'm afraid I'm not," I answered.

"Oh, yes, you are, you simply do not consciously realize it. In your own paintings, the constant use of the sun as a symbol and your bright colors are related to your lineage of ancient Mexican lifetimes, but the figures you use and the way you use circular form against form is due to the unconscious influence and contact with Giacometti. You influence others in the same way."

Later I found an art book which included many photographs of Giacometti's work, and was shocked. Although primarily sculpture, the similarity of figures, the use of negative space and form against form, was uncanny.

Still talking with Kandi, I asked, "David is obviously not a direct extension of yourself. You did not create him as a potential to explore, because you died well after he was born. Is it because you and he are an extension of the same exploration that you have the contact and affinity you now do? Just as Giacometti and I are an extension of the same exploration, or frequency?"

"Of course, my life was art, I will always love art, and can continue to explore through David. His belief system has expanded to the degree that he openly accepts me, and as long as he does, we can co-explore."

"How does all this relate to men and women returning or being born again to be together?"

"Well, it isn't a matter of returning, quite as you think of it, but what you are beginning to understand negates none of your previous beliefs. You are extensions of your creators, and their creators, and their creators. In reality you are one—individual identities, part of the whole and the whole, within a constant 'now.' But to answer your question more understandably, in the past, as you think of it, energy in the form of exploration was created by two identities. I am speaking symbolically to aid comprehension. That energy was not fully explored within one physical life, or two, or twenty, or whatever . . . so it continues to be the basis of an exploration of potential. One of many bases within the same exploration, I should say. You think of it as reincarnation, and you are not incorrect in this, but it is in reality through a lineage of individual identities. The past lives you and your loved one have experienced together in regression are quite valid, but did not exist within exactly the perspective you have perceived them."

"What about the existing ideas of karma?" I asked.

"This concept is part of a belief system—it exists and is valid as long as it is accepted—but belief systems, like everything else created in the mind, can be expanded and transcended. Beyond belief systems, all is nothing and nothing is everything."

"What is the goal?" I questioned.

"Whatever you make it. All identities should be free to explore whatever potentials they desire to explore, without others invading their belief systems. If you need a more complete answer I will sum it up in two words: *love* and *freedom*."

"This opens completely new doors of exploration. I have a million questions, and there are obviously many new areas of regressive hypnosis to experiment with. Will you help, Kandi?"

"Of course," he responded.

Donna and Bryan

"I WANT YOU TO GO BACK TO THE BEGINNING OF THE problems you are presently experiencing with your husband Bryan." Thirty-three-year-old Donna Morris was lying comfortably in the hypnosis lounger, in a deep trance. I had mentioned nothing about past lives, but had given her instructions to return to the initial confrontations with her husband.

Q. What do you see and what are you doing?
A. No . . . no . . . no . . . oh, please, no!
Q. I want you to speak up and tell me what is happening.
A. They're going to kill my son . . . they're going to . . . oh, no!
Q. Why are they going to do this? (Instructions given to calm the subject.)
A. It is the law . . . but they can't . . . oh . . .
Q. Has he done something wrong?
A. He is only six months old . . . no . . . it is the law. (Subject starts to cry, and further intensive instructions are given to look upon the situation only as an observer, without pain or emotion.)
Q. Now, very calmly I want you to explain to me why the law would do such a thing to a six-month-old baby?
A. All children considered to be potentially unfit . . . physically . . . are killed. My son has been sick, but

he'll be all right . . . he's not unfit . . . just because . . . oh . . . oh . . .

Q. Where do you live, what country?

A. Greece.

Q. Can you tell me about your social position?

A. We are Spartiates. . . . I understand . . . but it is so wrong . . . so unjust.

Q. Tell me more about what is happening.

A. They've taken him away.

Q. Who took him away?

A. Two soldiers.

Q. Upon whose instructions?

A. The council.

Q. Is there anyone there with you now?

A. Menelan. (Phonetic spelling.) My husband.

Q. What is his reaction to what has just transpired?

A. It is his fault . . . he agrees . . . he told them. . . . I HATE HIM! I HATE HIM!

The subject begins to scream. She is given calming instructions and removed from the past-life environment.

HISTORIC FOLLOW-UP NOTES:

Sparta was a town in Greece, and during the sixth century the privileged ruling class of Spartiates killed all infants who appeared physically inferior. This practice in time resulted in a dangerous shortage of population. At the age of seven all male children were taken by the state and raised to adulthood in an environment of rigorous military training.

Q. I want you to forget everything you have just experienced. Totally forget everything about your Grecian lifetime. I now want you to move forward in time, to another lifetime in which you and your present husband have been together, if indeed such a lifetime exists. It will be at the time of an important event that transpired between the two of you. (Instructions given.)

A. Ha-ha-ha-ha-ha-ha (deep laughter) . . . the Roman fool.

Q. Tell me what is happening.

A. I killed him.

Q. Why did you kill someone?

A. Why not? . . . My sword drips of his blood.

Q. Tell me who you are.

A. Patilina. (Phonetic spelling.)

Q. Where do you live?

A. Everywhere.

Q. What race are you?

A. We are Huns . . . what else?

Q. Why did you kill the Roman!

A. I kill all Romans.

Additional questioning showed that the man Patilina had killed had been Menelan in the Grecian lifetime.

HISTORIC FOLLOW-UP NOTES:

About 450 the Huns plundered and then collected tribute from the northern provinces of East Rome. Eventually defeated by a combined Roman and German army in 451, they retreated to Hungary.

Donna was instructed to move to another life, at the time of an important event, in which she and her husband had known each other.

A. He smiles at me.

Q. Who smiles at you?

A. The tall one . . . from another island.

Q. Tell me about what you are experiencing.

A. They came this morning on the sunrise.

Q. Have you seen them before?

A. No . . . the storm brought them.

Q. Are they friendly to your people?

A. Oh, yes . . . I like him.

Q. You are female, is that correct?

A. Yes.

Q. All right, let's move forward in time until something important happens between you and this man. (Instructions given.)

A. He's taking me to the boat . . . carrying me. (Concern in subject's voice.)

Q. Are you going willingly?

A. No . . . no . . . he's taking me . . . the others are asleep. . . . They're taking our things too . . . he has his hand over my mouth and I'm kicking . . . oh. . . . (Long pause.) He hit me on the head.

Q. What is happening now?

A. I'm just lying in the bottom of the boat . . . not moving.

Q. Let's move forward in time one month. (Instructions given.) What are you doing now?

A. Working . . . drying and spreading the leaves.

Q. Explain to me what has transpired in the last month.

A. He stole me . . . brought me to his island . . . many days . . . now I have to work with the others. They are very cruel.

Q. Did he take you for a mate?

A. No . . . just to work. He laughs at me.

Additional questioning uncovered no further lives in which they had been together, so the subject was given instructions to remember everything she had experienced, including the Grecian lifetime, and then awakened.

"If that is actually our past history . . . my God, we've only gotten back together to get each other," Donna said, rubbing her eyes in an attempt to return to present-day reality.

"To work it out is more like it, I'm afraid," I said.

Donna and her husband Bryan were separated at the time of the regression, November 1974. Their six-year marriage had been a monumental private war. They both earned an above-average income in their individual professions, Bryan as an insurance salesman, Donna a registered nurse. There were no children.

"What is the primary problem between you?" I asked, as we sat discussing the regression and the metaphysical aspect of relationships.

"You name it," she responded. "Everything . . . money, not the lack of it, but how we should spend it, sex, his relatives, my relatives, our friends, our time, . . . just everything. Sometimes I think the only reason we fight is because we like to fight. You have to have an excuse, you know!"

"Does it ever get physical?"

"No, thank God! He's come close to hitting me, but he never has. We just yell and scream at each other. I know I'm guilty of it too, but he does a million little things to purposely irritate me."

"Maybe you're beginning to mellow a bit then," I laughed. "At least you haven't gone after him with a sword this time."

In October 1975 I contacted Donna again. She explained to me that she and Bryan had reconciled at Christmastime, but were divorced the following spring. The parting was evidently achieved with a minimum of hostilities.

"After the regression I thought twice about everything I said to him," she explained. "I was paranoid about making it worse in any future lifetimes we may need to be together."

Trenna and Dick

THE FOLLOWING CASE HISTORY IS FROM MY OWN PERSONAL experience. I include it because it provides a cross-check that serves to add validity to the regression, and offers past-life explanations for present-day situations.

I had known Trenna for about a year and was very attracted to her from our first meeting. While working with the Hypnosis Center experiment, I taught an experimental class in "accelerated regressive hypnosis." Trenna was a natural, rapidly developing her abilities to the unique point of being able, in a limited way, to regress herself. We worked together on some experiments which proved to be extremely enlightening, but at the time we both had our own personal involvements. Several months later these had changed for both of us and we started seeing each other.

We talked about doing a regression to search out a past link, but never took the time. Then on a Sunday night in April 1974, while I was working in my studio, she lay down in the bedroom and went into self-hypnosis. A short time later she came into the studio and said, "I just had an experience I can't sort out . . . I saw myself as an Indian woman. It was sundown, I was waiting for a decision to be made, and I knew the people were against me. . . . I saw myself standing on a hill watching the sunset. The land was grassy with a lot of hills . . . it was cold. Then a tall Indian man walked up to me. I was wearing a necklace . . . he lifted it up to look at it closer . . . then together we walked down the hill and in front of all the people, he patted my stomach and made a gesture that showed me and the tribe it would be all right. We then went inside . . . I knew I was pregnant and I would be allowed to have the child."

I had been only half listening until she got to the part about the Indian man. . . . I remembered a personal reading with Kingdon Brown, the nationally known psychic, that had taken place in his home a couple of years before. I'd never talked about it because it didn't seem to have any particular importance . . . but now Trenna was telling me about an experience that I was already familiar with, and one of which she had absolutely no prior knowledge.

I was pretty sure the reading had been recorded, but it would be in storage with other related material at another location. There was no way to find it until the next day.

Regression is impossible to control in self-hypnosis, so we decided to do an actual session where I would induce the trance and direct the questions. In this way a subject can be easily guided and questioned. There is full control and safeguards, should a previous experience become traumatic to the subject. The following is a transcript of the regression tape made that night:

Trenna

First Regression Session

Hypnotic trance induced, regression instructions given to return to the Indian lifetime.

Q. Tell me what you see and what you are doing.
A. Sitting inside.
Q. Is there anyone else there with you?

A. A man.

Q. Can you describe him?

A. He's tall, he's sitting cross-legged. . . .

Q. Can you describe what he is wearing?

A. Animal skins.

Q. Are you talking?

A. Yes.

Q. Can you tell me what the conversation is about?

A. He's disappointed in me.

Q. Why?

A. (Long pause.) Something I did. (Emotion starts to build.)

Q. You are looking upon this situation only as an observer, without pain and without emotion. Now I want you to speak up and tell me what you did.

A. I was captured . . . captured by enemies. . . .

Q. I want you to tell me how this happened . . . see it in your own mind and tell me how it happened.

A. All the men were gone . . . I was cooking . . . they came in . . . they took me. . . .

Q. How is it that you are back here now?

A. I ran away.

Q. How can the person you are talking with be disappointed in you if you were captured, you had no choice?

A. I'm pregnant.

Q. Is he disappointed because you were raped?

A. Yes.

Q. What would he have had you do?

A. (Strong emotional reaction and tears.) Kill myself.

Q. (Instructions given to calm subject down; she is told to rise above the emotions.) Let's move forward in time until the decision is made to allow you to keep the baby. (Instructions given.)

Q. I want you to tell me now about the decision and about the feelings of the people.

A. I'm looked upon with shame.

Q. By all the people?

A. Yes . . . except he . . . he understands more.

Q. Can you tell me his name?

A. Chezta. (Phonetic spelling.)

Q. Is Chezta the one who is in the position to make the decision as to whether or not you will be allowed to keep the child?

A. Yes.

Q. All right—tell me about the decision.

A. He wants me to keep it.

Q. All right, let's move forward in time again, to the time of birth of the child. (Instructions given.) Tell me what is happening.

A. I've had the baby . . . it's a boy.

Q. Tell me now about the situation you are living in.

A. I live with Chezta.

Q. Has he taken you as his wife?

A. Uh-huh.

Q. Does he feel good about the birth of the child?

A. Well . . . yes . . . but apprehensive.

Q. You were not married before you were captured, is that correct?

A. We were to be . . .

Q. I want you to move forward in time now, to an important event. I will let your subconscious mind choose an important event that will take place in the future in regard to you and your child. (Instructions given.) What do you see and feel now?

A. Proud.

Q. Proud about what?

A. The boy is being honored for his bravery.

Q. How old is he now?

A. He's grown.

Q. What did he do?

A. He warned the tribe.

Q. I want you now to describe the country that you live in.

A. Tall grass, hills, and rocks.

Q. Does it get cold enough to snow there?

A. Rains.

Q. I want you to tell me the name of your people, your tribe?

A. Kytecs. (Phonetic spelling.)

Q. I want you to move forward in time to the last day of your life in this incarnation we are examining. You will feel no pain, you will not yet have crossed over into spirit, but it will be the last day of your life. (Instructions given.) Tell me now, what you are doing. What is the situation?

A. My son has children.

Q. What are you doing at this time?

A. In front of the fire.

Q. Are you very old?

A. Uh-huh.

Q. What about your husband?

A. He's there.

Q. Have you had a happy life together?

A. Yes.

Q. Did you have any other children?

A. No.

Q. I want you now to look back over your life . . . you have the power and ability to do this. I want you to tell me about the most important thing that happened in your life. (Instructions given.)

A. My son being accepted . . . it took so long . . . so long.

(End of this portion of past-life regression.)

Kingdon Brown's Psychic Reading

The next day I found the tape recording of the reading which took place in Kingdon Brown's home in May 1972, two years before I met Trenna. Trenna knew nothing of this tape, but her regression confirmed the events told to me by Kingdon Brown. Throughout the session Brown kept picking up impressions of an Indian woman and child. He saw the child as a fetus in the womb and later as a baby on the woman's back. The images would fade in and out, and he didn't understand the meaning of what he was receiving. Then during the last twenty minutes he made contact with one of my guides, and several past lives were covered . . . among them was this information, which is transcribed exactly as it was received:

. . . the Indian woman and the child . . . there is something very important about this. . . . It's not clear to me . . . the peaceful sort of Flagstaff background (mountains and forest area in northern Arizona) . . . a natural kind of inner peace . . . serenity. . . . You were associated with a group of people— what would now be Mexico. . . . This is a group of people who lived in adobe . . . apartments. . . . There are a lot of people there, and I see a man, tall man who wears. . . . Ah, the weather must be cool, it looks like it must be a blanket or robe of some kind . . . it's completely around him. . . . He's walking back and forth . . . and the sun is going down in the distance and it's a purple cloud color . . . and he must decide . . . (Long pause.) . . . whether the child shall live . . . (Very long pause.) . . . Now I'm getting what it is . . . it's an odd thing . . . there's a child about to be born . . . but there's a question as to whether the child shall live or not . . . or be born or not . . . at first as I touched on it, it seemed as though there was a question about the child versus the mother . . . but that's not the case . . . there's something about the child . . . whether the child should be permitted to live, for some reason. . . . There's a question about this, as though the child might not be . . . and you are making the decision . . . and it seems to be the decision is made to let the child live, but this is in opposition to the code, or the pressure of the community . . . for some reason I don't know why . . . the child ordinarily would not be permitted to live . . . there is something about that child. . . . Now the child is not the daughter you have now. . . . This question of the living or the death of a child is critical to your karmic pattern. . . . It may even be so in another form in this life . . . the power over the decision . . . and you go ahead and say . . . well, yes . . . but the pressure is on you not to permit the child to be born. . . . There's something symbolically tied in with this . . . because it's coming in from a different . . . (Pause.) . . . from your line . . . that one's coming in directly from your karmic pattern . . .

(End of this portion of the recording)

(Note: Kingdon Brown is a highly respected and nationally known psychic, who has written several major metaphysical books. He is a personal friend and we have worked on unusual psychic cases together. His "readings" are done in a light trance state and preceded by a prayer in which he asks for guidance and information that would prove to be of value to the entity for whom he is conducting the reading. He is one of the featured psychics in the book *Revelation—The Divine Fire* by Brad Stieger.)

In August 1974 Trenna and I made the decision to live together. She had no children by her first marriage, but by the end of August, due to an unusual set of circumstances, it became necessary and desirable for my oldest son, from my first marriage, to come and live with us.

In March 1975 we decided to do another regression session in search of additional past-life ties.

Trenna

Second Regression Session

Upon the induction of hypnosis and the completion of the regression preparation and instructions, Trenna saw us together riding in an old cart. This time we were uneducated peasants, again in our present male-female roles, and as a man and wife living in the town of Marseilles on the southeast coast of France, in the early 1700s. The lifetime was drab, dirty, and depressing.

In my thirties I lost my job working in an open-air market in the town. The times were extremely hard, and without work we moved through the countryside, living however we could. We had two children, a boy and a girl, both of whom died at a young age in a plague. Eventually we discovered an abandoned farmhouse and moved in, spending the rest of our days eking out a living off the land.

After carrying her through death and into spirit, I found that she maintained a bitterness about the lifetime she had just experienced. "I don't know why my children had to die so young," was more a statement than a question. When she was calmer, I asked her why she had to live such a lifetime, what she had needed to learn. "I needed to learn humility through experiencing a life of poverty and ignorance," was her answer.

When awakened, Trenna felt depressed about what she had just relived. "It was awful, just awful," she said with disgust. "Everything was soot-covered in the town, the people seemed miserable. I could see us riding along in an old cart, the kind with solid round wheels. When you carried me to the last day of my life, I saw myself just sitting on the stones in front of a fireplace . . . you'd been dead for about five years, and all I wanted to do was die. I couldn't read or write, and I was old . . . and I could hardly take care of myself. I can't believe how depressing it was."

HISTORIC FOLLOW-UP NOTES:

The town of Marseilles existed at this time on the southeast coast of France, and does to this day. It had been the birthplace of the Black Plague a few hundred years before, and smallpox was a problem of major proportions in the early 1700s. These years were just prior to the French revolution and were extremely hard times for the peasant population.

We later completed a third and fourth regression. In one we found ourselves in revolutionary times, successfully fighting an oppressive situation. The other was a lifetime of spiritual involvement in which, although we were together for only a short period of time, we seemed to achieve a level of higher understanding.

Alamos:
A Group Reincarnation

INDIVIDUALS ARE BORN AGAIN TO BE TOGETHER WITHIN the same time frame, to explore their individual and combined potentials. The same is often true of groups of individuals, and one of the best ways to illustrate how this works is through my own experience, which has been verified through numerous channels.

This book, or rather the concepts expressed within it, was written by myself and many, many others, thousands of years ago in sequential time as we judge it. The concepts in this volume and in books which will follow it are being presented once again as part of a group or tribal plan. Only recently have I become fully aware of the unseen guidance and preparation that has occurred prior to its beginnings.

Trenna and I arrived in the mountain town of Alamos, Sonora, on a rainy afternoon. It was too wet to camp out comfortably, so we checked into a local hotel. No sooner had we arrived in our room than an uneasy feeling came over me. I wanted to walk—consciously I didn't know where, never having been in the town before, but subconsciously I seemed to know. Moving quickly through the dirt streets and back alleys, into the poorest section of the town and through it, we arrived at a walled cemetery. Tears welled up in my eyes, and I literally lost control, crying, experiencing intense emotions and not knowing why. Trenna was supportive but mystified.

When we returned to the hotel, my emotions calmed, but the uneasy feeling remained. The next day I returned to the cemetery alone. Containing the emotional reaction to a degree, I crisscrossed the graves and monuments, searching for one that might have a particular meaning, but discovered nothing.

We camped outside Teotihuacán, one of the largest ruins in Mexico, so as to allow a sunrise exploration of the ancient city. Both Trenna and I felt drawn to this particular site, although recorded history knows little of its origin. It was deserted and overgrown when the Aztecs arrived in Mexico. The famous "Street of the Dead" was so named by the Aztecs, for they felt the huge mounds were the burial sites of gods.

The entire day was spent probing the structures, both of us feeling an excitement and fascination that were overwhelming. Before nightfall we were back on the road north; preoccupied with the events of the day, discussing Teotihuacán, we drove until exhausted. We arrived quite late at La Mansion, a luxury hotel in the middle of nowhere, and enjoyed a quiet dinner and swim in the pool. Upon returning to our room, I lay down and immediately seemed to drift into a trance. Vivid images came into my mind—I was no longer in a hotel room, but back in Teotihuacán once more, only the city was not in ruins. It was a magnificent center alive with thousands of people. It was night, yet everything was immersed in light. A huge fire burned on the top of the Pyramid of the Moon, and elegantly robed men lined the steps from top to bottom.

Trenna related later that I began tossing and talking. She was now quite familiar with trances, and psychic experiences were no longer mystifying. She began to question me quietly. "What are you experiencing?" she asked.

"They're all here, all of them. . . . I'm in the center of the ring at the base. . . . Everyone is looking at me. . . . He's talking to me. . . . I don't understand. . . . I don't even know what you're talking about!"

"What are they saying to you?" she questioned.

"I don't know about any books . . . how do I find the books when I don't even know about them? I'm supposed to get the books together, and I haven't done it. The man standing halfway up the pyramid keeps telling me . . . it's like I'm on trial . . . they're all expecting me to get the books together."

I came out of the trance in a cold sweat. Trenna was sitting on the other side of the bed with eyes like saucers. "Good God," she said. "What in the world was that all about?"

"I don't know. I feel like a child who's just been reprehended. That has to be the most vivid vision I've ever received. I'm supposed to find the books. It's my assignment and I've blown it . . . I guess? I don't have the faintest idea what the hell they were talking about. Probably something that happened in a past life, and our visit simply allowed subconscious memories to come to the surface."

Feeling fully awake, we discussed the experience in detail but were unable to arrive at any other meaningful conclusions. I am knowledgeable of a reincarnational pattern of lifetimes in what is now called Mexico, yet this experience did not tie in with any previous awareness. Within a few days, lacking additional information, we more or less forgot the incident.

In August an old friend called. "Dick, this is Ed Kaye, how in the hell are you doing?" I hadn't heard from him in months. While in Phoenix on business I had tried several times, unsuccessfully, to reach him. An invitation to attend a weekend-long Fourth of July party had been returned marked, "Moved—no forwarding address."

We exchanged greetings and a rapid-fire updating of the events that had transpired over the months we'd had no contact. "I'm moving to Prescott," he said. "I'd heard you were up here, but I wasn't sure. Do you know of any rental available out in the woods, where I can live and set up shop?"

I told him to come on out to our house and plan to use it as a base of operations until he found a place of his own. Ed arrived with a beautiful girl named Phyllis, whom he was now living with. They had met in Philadelphia. She was on vacation from Florida, and Ed was there on business from Arizona. The attraction was immediate, and a series of unusual events had drawn them together in Phoenix shortly thereafter. Phyllis had a background as a special education teacher who worked in a black ghetto in Miami. She now hoped to find similar work with the Indians around Prescott.

During the course of the weekend much of the conversation was about regressive hypnosis, for I had just finished the first draft of this book. Although I had never discussed my metaphysical activities or psychic involvement with Ed prior to that time, both he and Phyllis were extremely receptive. They wanted to experience regression, so Sunday night we decided to do a session.

After the trance was induced and regression preparation completed, I instructed Ed to return to a meaningful prior existence. I let his own subconscious mind choose a lifetime that might prove beneficial to his present understanding. When instructed to return to an important event in this past life, he saw himself with another man tearing up manuscripts and hiding them in the crack of a huge stone, which made up part of the wall of a pyramid. Further questioning revealed that he was in ancient Mexico and that I was the man with him. He later explained, "It didn't look like you do now, but it was you. . . . I knew it."

Before awakening Ed, I maneuvered him to the higher-self God level of his own superconscious mind. "From the perspective you have now attained you have the ability to look down upon your present life with an expanded awareness. I want you to open yourself to receive information that will prove valuable to you in the present. I will not question you during this time, but you will receive this information and you will consciously remember it upon awakening."

Trenna poured coffee while Ed attempted to grasp the magnitude of what he had just experienced. "I've never been through anything like that in my life . . . WOW! I don't believe it. It was so real. I was there, man. . . . I don't believe it!"

We discussed the regression, and I inquired about the higher-self aspect of the session. "Did you receive any information that you consciously recall?"

"Yeah . . . but it didn't make any sense. I just kept hearing this voice saying, 'Get the books together, get the books together, get the books together.' I don't know anything about any damn books."

September 10, 1975: David and Lynda Paladin were invited to our house for dinner. About a half-hour before they arrived, Ed and Phyllis dropped in. They had just moved their first load of furniture from Phoenix to a nearby mountain cabin they had rented. Trenna had fixed enough Chimichangas for an army, so we invited them to stay for dinner. I was anxious for Ed to meet David.

After dinner, conversation turned to the subject of Mexico. David's affinity for the country parallels my own, and we all exchanged tales of our experiences there. I mentioned that I loved Alamos, Sonora, explaining that I felt it was one of the most beautiful towns in Mexico.

David responded, "I agree with you, but I had an experience there that took me a while to get over. The cemetery on the edge of town, are you familiar with it?"

"Oh, yes," I said, goose pimples popping up all over my body.

"Well, I completely broke down there," he said. "I went to pieces, and they had to literally carry me out of the place . . . taking me to the local seeress. She worked for a while at calming me down, and I explained that I saw an old white church on the site. There is no such structure there now.

"She then explained the situation. There had indeed at the time of the Spanish conquest been just such a structure on the site. As the Spanish moved north through Mexico they attempted conversion of the Indians to Christianity. In what is now Alamos, they found a tribe of Indians that resisted conversion. All attempts failed and the Spanish proceeded to exert force. They castrated the men, cut out tongues and poked out their eyes, but to no avail. In the end they murdered five hundred natives and buried them in a mass grave. Immediately following this execution, Spanish soldiers began dying for no obvious reason. 'Dropping like flies,' she said. As a form of exorcism, they placed the Christian graveyard on top of the Indian burial site to quiet the evil spirits. Naturally the original shrine was removed."

I sat on the floor in front of the fireplace, shocked, looking at David. My own experience in Alamos flooded through my mind, and the words of a 1972 life reading by my friend Kingdon Brown (the same reading which included the information in the previous chapter) pulled more of the pieces together. The pertinent part of the tape is transcribed here:

"You were part of a large group, or tribe, who have reincarnated together again and again . . . but you were all wiped out . . . all wiped out at once. I don't understand, for I do not believe it was a natural calamity, but you all died together. In this life you are reuniting once again in Arizona. You have already met many of this group, and you will continue over the next few years to meet many more. They are coming from all over the country and yours is a common bond and tie. Great strength can be achieved through this union."

Our conversation now drifted into the discussion of metaphysical concepts. At one point I asked David a very difficult question . . . he sat back in contemplation, and a totally different voice answered me. "Would you mind an interruption from an old friend?" he said in English but with a heavy Russian accent. On my response, he provided an in-depth explanation to my question.

I was talking directly with Wassily Kandinsky again. For the next hour and a half we asked Kandi involved questions, which he easily and eloquently answered. Then he said he would bid us good evening.

September 13, 1975: Trenna and I were invited over to the Paladins' for dinner along with one of our close friends and neighbors, Peggy Weisman, one of David's art students. David was busy in the kitchen preparing the dinner when we arrived, and we all secretly hoped that we were about to experience another of the Paladins' paranormal occurrences.

David often goes to the grocery store and finds himself at the check stand with numerous items he has no conscious recollection of having picked up. He accepts this quite naturally, for the entities who use him as a channel also often cook unusual meals for the family and guests.

We all sat down at the table to a great salad, and the dinner conversation was about everyday activities. Then David returned to the kitchen, emerging with individual plates of what looked to be a gourmet delight. Trenna asked him what it was, and a totally new voice answered her. "It is a meal of sixteenth-century India, madam," he said very softly. I looked at David; his head was down, and he appeared extremely shy and unwilling to look up. We were speaking to Zahad, one of the identities who talks through Paladin. He went on to explain the unique ingredients combined with rice. "Pecans were worth a man's life in my time," he said. The main course was deboned chicken, stuffed with shrimp and covered with a curry sauce. I had never eaten a more delicious meal.

After dinner we all discussed various directions and approaches to a book I was considering writing about David's unbelievable but true psychic adventures. Kandi came in and out of the conversation, offering advice and presenting concepts. As analogies to make his points, some of the information was directly in regard to those of us in the room, and we found our heads swimming with almost more than we could comprehend.

Later in the evening all the related occurrences of the past year came to mind, and I addressed myself to Kandi. "Can you provide me with any insight as to the psychic occurrences in Mexico which David and I have both experienced? Also do you know anything about some ancient books I'm supposed to find and get together?"

"I'm surprised you haven't figured it out on your own," Kandi replied. "What you are now doing and the concepts which we have been discussing over the last several weeks are the basis of the books. You have already begun. In your Teotihuacán incarnation you had this knowledge. It was recorded and also painted upon the walls of the structure which stood adjacent to the Pyramid of the Sun. Changes in governing structures caused you to fear the misuse of this knowledge, just as you do again now, so in the past you painted over the murals, disguising their true meanings, and you and others destroyed the records. David was part of this, as was Edward and your young lady." (He meant Trenna.) "There were many others whom you have met and will continue to meet. You had far more knowledge at that time than you have thus far assimilated in your present life, but you are rapidly opening yourself once again. A pact was made, in what is now called Teotihuacán, agreeing that you would re-assemble every seven hundred years to present this information once again. You have reincarnated together many times, but the conditions have not always been conducive to the presentation of these concepts. It is time once more to offer this understanding to those who have the ability to perceive it."

I sat on the couch, stunned, unable to ask more. It wasn't necessary, anyway. All the seeming unrelated events of the past years had been pulled together within five minutes.

In the days that followed, Trenna and I pieced together many more related occurrences that had led from the past to the present. I could see how everything that happened, from the time I left school, had been channeled toward my present work—contacts with publishers, the gradual swing from art to psychic research and writing, even down to the poetry books I'd written. Poetry is a matter of taking an idea, situation, or emotion and boiling it down to its simplest and most easily communicable form. That was certainly the task I was now confronted with in expressing metaphysical concepts.

September 20, 1975: Desmond Williams, who is the subject of one of the case histories, knocked on our front door, accompanied by a photographer from the Scottsdale

Progress newspaper. A reporter who was interested in doing a study on me had stayed overnight with us two weeks before. He had arrived a disbeliever, experienced regression, and had gone home a bit confused. The photographer was there to do a follow-up, and Desmond had come along for the ride.

I'd seen him only twice in the last year, and it was good to get an update on his own activities and his involvement with the Phoenix psychic movement, which he keeps in close touch with. During our discussion I mentioned some of what we'd been experiencing. At the mention of David's and my own experience in Alamos, Mexico, Desmond reacted intensely, before I could explain the details. "I feel sick," he said. "My head just started to pound, and if I don't lie down I think I'll throw up. It may sound weird, but I don't even want you to talk about that."

I flashed upon what had upset him as it happened, but decided to wait until later to verify my ideas. After dinner we discussed doing a regression, and Desmond was willing. "I know what you're looking for, and if it's reality, I'm almost afraid to have to see it," he said.

Desmond

Past Life Regression

September 1975

I was already familiar with Desmond's trance ability, so induction of hypnosis was achieved quickly. Regression preparation was completed and the following instructions given: "If you experienced a lifetime in which you were in any way connected with events which took place as part of the Spanish Conquest of Mexico in what is now known as Alamos, Sonora, I want you to return to the time you first found yourself in this area." (Instructions given.)

Q. What do you see and what are you doing?
A. I am in a small village . . . I'm a priest.
Q. Describe yourself to me, your physiscal appearance.
A. I have on a brown robe . . . I wear a beard.
Q. Are there others with you now?
A. Yes, I am part of the contingency of priests who came over for the conversions.

Additional questions showed that many Spanish soldiers were part of the expedition, and that he was unhappy with the circumstances surrounding the conquest. "The priests are acting like savage animals in the name of God," he said. Tears now started to run out of Desmond's closed eyes, and his body began to shiver and tremble almost to the point of convulsions. Strong suggestions would mitigate the physical reactions for a few moments, but then they would return. Bob, the photographer who was observing the regression, could not mentally handle Desmond's experience and had to get up and go outside until it was finished.

Q. What is happening within the village?
A. We have built pens . . . from poles of wood . . . the Indians have been placed inside them. As is the custom, since we arrived in New Spain, if they will not be converted they must die.
Q. How are you attempting to convert them?
A. We order them to accept Christ as their savior . . . but they have no idea what we are talking about . . . they're ignorant people. . . . They don't understand why they should worship one God when they worship everything.
Q. Are you succeeding in the conversion of any of the Indians?
A. No, for they do not understand brutality . . . they don't understand how God could kill.

As the regression progressed Desmond saw the Monseigneur order him to kill some of the Indians, and when
he refused, he was arrested. According to his account, the
priests were as savage and brutal as the soldiers. "I don't
mind the physical hardship, being away from the place
that I love . . . having to march and act as a soldier," he
said. "But these people were not prepared for what happened. Many of the tribes we've encountered have been
warriors and have put up a fight . . . but these people
don't understand the idea of fighting. They are defense-
less."

Q. Did you march into their village and immediately
   begin conversion?
A. No, not at first . . . first we established friendly feelings. . . . Our encampment was well outside their
   village.
Q. How did they initially react to you?
A. They welcomed us . . . they fed us . . . and treated us
   as if we were one of their own race. . . . After a few
   months the order was issued to begin indoctrination.
Q. When did the killing begin?
A. Just as examples . . . to encourage conversion . . . but
   it worked the other way.
Q. What have you done to the people?
A. Children have been impaled upon stakes . . . and left
   to die . . . they've had their heads cut off . . . women
   have been mutilated . . . sexually by the soldiers with
   the blessings of the priests . . . who took great pleasure
   in this.
Q. I want to move forward in time to the completion
   of your stay in this area. I want you to see every
   detail of what is happening and verbally communicate
   it to me. By reexperiencing this event you can rise
   above it, and relieve yourself of its prior influence.
   (Instructions given.)
A. I see men they have set on fire . . . soldiers are standing around laughing. . . . Two soldiers have just raped
   an Indian woman and now are cutting her body with
   their swords . . . dismembering her . . . throwing

pieces of her body into one of the fires. . . . Some soldiers on horseback . . . with lances . . . are running everybody down, even children. . . . There is a pavilion . . . the Monseigneur is sitting upon a ceremonial throne which was brought from Spain . . . he is surrounded by priests . . . there seems to be no order in what is happening . . . except for the fires . . . cruelty. . . .

Q. How many Indians are now left alive?

A. Of the six hundred and forty-eight, some escaped, but I'm sure that among those we retained, there can be no more than ten left alive.

At this point in the regression the subject completely broke down, screaming and sobbing. "I can't take any more . . . oh, please, I can't take any more."

September 22, 1975: Desmond called from Phoenix to tell me what had occurred in a past-life circle (described in the next chapter) Sunday night. "I was terrified to sit in on the session," he said. "There were about fifteen people there, and I feared the memory of Alamos experience would come out again, and sure enough it did. Only first as an experience on the boat from Spain to Mexico. This same situation had been picked up two weeks earlier by a couple of women in the group, but I hadn't related the situation to myself. Often one person will receive and others in the group will be able to tap in on the visual impressions. Anyway Sunday night this came in again, and we followed it all the way to the massacre in Alamos. Six or seven people received identical images, and Gil [Dr. Gil Gilly, a well-known psychic, author, and TV personality] tapped in to verify the situation. He said it was very real and carried unusually strong vibrations."

September 23, 1975: By now I was well into a series of biweekly sessions with David Paladin to gather material for a potential book. Every Tuesday and Thursday we spend two or three hours in his studio, tape-recording rap sessions. Much of the time is spent allowing the various discarnate entities who speak through him to express themselves. Much of what we are receiving is totally new information, which transcends metaphysical concepts without negating them.

On this particular Tuesday morning, while in contact with Kandi, I asked him a question about the Teotihuacán group in an effort to understand a complicated theory he was explaining.

"Kandi, why did this group make such a commitment? And if we did, how could an idea from one lifetime carry over for so many thousand years, assuming, as you say, that Teotihuacán actually dates back much further than the currently accepted geological dating of 200 B.C.?"

Historically the origin of Teotihuacán is unknown. No one is aware of who the people were, where they came from, or what language they spoke. It is believed that the civilization had ceased to exist five hundred years before the arrival of the Aztecs, who, upon discovering the already overgrown structures, believed them to be the burial places of gods. Carbon dating reveals that the city flourished from approximately 200 B.C. to 650 A.D., but Kandi had informed us that our radio carbon methods of dating history are very inaccurate, for we use today's standards as the basis, while in the past the situation on earth was quite different.

"There is enough energy remaining alive at this time for you to work with. The people feed a tremendous amount of energy into this idea," Kandi answered.

"But why?"

"Something happened you felt disastrous. Part of your belief system was being eliminated, and you wanted the wisdom to last for eternity. Not knowing that it would last for eternity anyway, you put even more energy into it, creating another potential from that experience."

There is no way to end this chapter, for I know as a group experience it is only beginning to be written. Some of those who share this Teotihuacán heritage, as explorations of the original potential, have been drawn together for the purpose of perpetuating an ancient energy. There may be many groups around the world which have evolved from the same source, and there are thousands of other groups with similar goals.

In Prescott and Groom Creek we are involved in individual and joint channels of exploration and discovery. The results are manifesting themselves in varying ways, and we all benefit from the activities and share in the knowledge. We do not expect anyone else to accept our concepts, but we release them after lengthy exploration, for consideration.

Past Lives Through Other Windows

WE ARE NOW EXPERIENCING THE DEATH PANGS OF THE Piscean Age, through the international, national, and personal turmoil of the day. But even as this is transpiring, a new wave of thinking is developing throughout the world. As we experience the death of the old materialistic and industrialized society, we are at the same time encountering the birth pangs of a new technological and altruistic Aquarian Age. This transitional time will be one of the necessary cleansing and great tests for many souls now living upon the earth.

I believe that as we advance into a new age, those who have evolved upward, raising their level of consciousness over many lifetimes, will once again find understanding in the Universal Truth. The recognition of past lives will become common knowledge, and telepathic communication will once again become a natural fact of life.

To evolve we must learn, and learning is a process of remembering the past. If we can become aware of negative karmic patterns in the past, this knowledge might help us to avoid similar mistakes in the future. The mind is conditioned to forget pain, but if we desire to take conscious control of our destiny, we must remember everything.

A conscious knowledge of our past through the recall of prior incarnations is an obvious channel for insight as to proper pathways in the future. As an example, I am aware of a past pattern of involvement with revolutions and the military, the most recent being a captain in the French Foreign Legion. The majority of my adult life was spent in upper Africa fighting the Arab people of that region. I have re-experienced this myself in regression, and since childhood have received mental flashes of a hand pulling back the bolt of a machine gun.

On several occasions, even prior to this knowledge, I've attended parties which have included Arab guests. Each time an uneasiness has come over me, and I've found myself moving to a corner of the room, with my back against the wall. The last time this occurred I also, once again, received the flashes of the hand on the gun.

Because I am aware of the past, I know how easy it would be for me to become involved in revolutionary activities . . . which would be a mistake. The use of violence solves nothing, and at the same time creates negative karma. An esoteric astrologer recently looked at my chart, and her first words were, "It would be very natural for you to take command in military situations. You have a past history of this and should avoid similar activity in this life."

Through the recall of the past I am also aware of positive patterns of aesthetic involvements with art, writing, and spiritual endeavors. These pathways, which lead in the proper direction, also come easy to me, because I've known them before.

There are numerous channels available to those who desire to find out about their own past. If you feel that seeking this understanding would be beneficial to your own soul's growth, I'm sure you will be properly guided to a source if you actively search one out. I personally favor recall techniques which allow an individual to see his own past, but there are also other valid windows to yesterday.

Hypnosis and Meditation

Directed hypnosis has already been thoroughly discussed in this book, but self-hypnosis and meditation are channels for self-induced visual exploration. Both require a period of training and dedication but are certainly worthy of consideration by the seeker of past-life knowledge. It would take far too much space to explain the methods of development in these pages, but there are numerous books already on the market, and classes are available in most cities of any size.

Special classes on regressive hypnosis are available in some areas, and at the Wáki Center (pronounced "Wa-ah-ki") in the mountains above Prescott, Arizona, we offer seminars in regression and accelerated regressive self-hypnosis.

I recently met with Don Weldon of Creative Guidelines, in Phoenix. Don teaches a twelve-week course in metaphysics and regression which he calls a Time Travel Class. In comparing notes, we both agreed that virtually anyone who actively desires a regressive experience and is willing to work toward achieving it will accomplish his goal.

Esoteric Astrology

Astrology, in the hands of a "true professional," is close to being an absolute science. You can accurately learn of your past, present, and future through this channel, but there are few working astrologers, in my opinion, who can be classified in this category. The real pros are very intelligent individuals who have usually devoted most of their adult life to the dedication and study of their craft.

Hazel Mooney of Scottsdale, Arizona, is considered the most respected esoteric astrologer in the Southwest.

I went to see her for two reasons. A very critical aspect in my daughter Jessi's chart was brought to my attention by an astrologer friend. I consider him very good, but I desired to have it read on a higher level. Through Hazel's abilities, working with Jessi's chart and the charts of her mother and me, a plan was developed to mitigate what could be a life-and-death aspect. Through studying the interactions, strengths, and weaknesses of the three charts, a protective aspect was uncovered, and the most appropriate location and companion for the child, during the critical three days, was established.

Hazel had no sooner picked up my chart than she told me of a past-life karmic career pattern. I told her she was exactly right, as had been verified through hypnotic regressions and psychic friends. I also wanted to talk with Hazel about my work on this book, and since "esoteric astrology" goes much deeper into the spiritual and into past incarnations than normal astrology, I asked her how often she would see prior-life involvement in the charts of lovers or married couples. "Ninety-five per cent of the time," she responded.

"I do three charts, a natal, progressed, and event chart," she explained. "If the ties are there, they will show up. But let me digress for just a moment . . . remember that astrology is not a 'causal' science—we don't use cause and effect, from our standpoint, to establish the scientific basis. We are concerned primarily with the logical sequence of events, so it is basically a timing mechanism. Now the extension of pure logic would imply, based upon the analogy, 'as above, so below' . . . consequently, 'as the past, so the future.' So we are at a crystallized moment in time in the present life. Therefore you can only draw on the past to implement the future."

We discussed at great length how she reads various chart aspects, and we covered enough interesting case histories to fill a book. Astrology is this fine lady's entire life, and through her work she has provided many hundreds of people with insight into their past, and thus their present . . . and using her talent and abilities, she offers guidance for the future.

Psychics, Channel Mediums and
Akashic Record Readers

If someone else informs you of your past lives, it is obviously important to establish the credence of the reader. There are many excellent psychics and channel mediums, there are more who are mediocre, and the charlatans abound in ever-increasing numbers.

I know many established psychics, whom I sincerely respect, who have more often than not provided me with valid data about my own past, present, and future. Yet I would never expect one hundred per cent accuracy from any of them.

Be extra-careful of channel mediums, for the knowledge they are providing is coming from the other side. The question is, from how highly evolved an entity? The lower forces are also capable of using some channels for a voice. I've observed good mediums in tune with positive sources, and I've seen many schizophrenics simply looking for attention.

As a general rule, beware of "red hand" readers (those with the sign of a red hand in front of their establishment) and séances. In a séance, if there is one individual present with a low level of consciousness, they can bring with them low-level entities.

There are several Akashic records readers around the country. There again I would attempt to establish their credence before consulting them. The Reverend Noel Street of Miami, who is a psychic healer and reader of the Akasa, has done readings for a hundred thousand people, and from what I know of his work, he has helped a great number through guidance in karmic and spiritual development, vocational areas, marital relationships, and past-life skills.

The Ouija Board and Pendulum

As a general rule I do not advocate the Ouija Board or the use of the pendulum for spiritual contact or guidance unless those using these mediums have a high level of awareness and understanding in metaphysical matters. It is often quite easy for a lower entity to come through an unprotected individual, especially if they are "sensitives," as many people are without realizing it. But the fact is, these media of communication are also channels for past-life information, and if used correctly and preceded by protectory techniques, can often be enlightening.

I feel compelled at this point to offer a couple of strong suggestions, should you attempt to seek knowledge in this way. First say a prayer, asking for protection while using the channel. Ask that only your own guides and spiritual Masters or loving entities of positive intent be allowed to come through or in any way to influence the information you receive. Then imagine a bright white light of protection surrounding your body. When you create this mentally, although you can't see it, it becomes real and provides an effective defense screen against lower astral interference. This is an ancient metaphysical protectory technique, and although you may not totally comprehend its effectiveness, please believe me that by evoking it you will be on much more positive ground.

A primary consideration in such matters is your own level of consciousness. If it is very high, you probably wouldn't need such protection; if it is extremely low, you'll probably need more than is included here.

If you should ever start to receive obscene language, talk of death or other negatives, stop working with the board or pendulum immediately. Powerful lower entities on the other side can play all sorts of games with your head . . . but only if you let them. I know of the case of a man in Phoenix who started receiving very spiritual information through the Ouija Board, but the advice soon turned to suggestions about his present life. As an example, he was told that he was too good for his present job, and that he should quit. In time, by following the advice he was receiving through the board, he literally ruined his life.

Although when I first became involved with metaphysics many years ago, I had several negative encounters with the board, I also found out some startling facts about my own past lives which were later verified through other channels.

Automatic or Direct Writing

Automatic writing, the technique of sitting relaxed, pencil in hand, while you quiet your mind to allow a contact to come through the pencil, is another valid channel for knowledge from the past. The same warnings and protectory techniques as described for the Ouija Board are apropos here.

Some people use a typewriter in the same way, and often information can come through when you least expect it. Trenna's first experience occurred while she was typing a manuscript for me. She had just placed a clean sheet of paper into the typewriter, placed her hands on the keys, and her hands seemed to take off by themselves. When she looked up, it stopped; when she looked away, it continued to come through. The following is what she received:

```
You now have learned, and last night
you were instructed as to the ways of
the old. You will continue learning
and receiving the data, as you are
ready for it. You are right in assuming
that the material in the Jane Robert's
book [author's note: The Education of
Oversoul 7/The Seth Material] is very
close to the instructions you have
been receiving, thinking it from outer
```

spaces. It actually is from the
innermost you. The God you. There are
many others who are in essence me, the
one you call upon in time of need.
You may try to reach me through
hypnosis, but your primary learning will
come from your dreams. The more you try
to remember, the more you will be able
to perceive. Don't keep looking behind
doors, it will come to you when you are
ready. There are many around you who
may try to deter you from the teaching,
don't let their sense of values
destroy your path to your inner being.
Now let this be all for now, I will
come to you later. Continue your work,
your reading. The contacts you have
made so far are on the right path.
Remember me and I will be there, you
are as you create . . .

The first contact with automatic writing is often disturbing to the receiver, but it can be a beautiful experience, and if allowed to develop can become a path to enlightenment.

Several times while writing the last section of this book I had trouble finding the proper words to communicate my ideas. When this was the case, I went into a light trance, asked for higher help, then blanked my mind while laying my fingers on the typewriter keyboard. Every time the words came through quickly and effortlessly.

My sister-in-law, Ilah, lives with her husband Bob and their two children in Excelsior, Minnesota. She has received extremely interesting information through automatic writing. Ilah is a college graduate and is very much involved with and works for the local Presbyterian church. They live a very normal life and are quite dedicated to their own religion, yet because of psychic events they've experienced, they have become much more interested in occult understanding.

Ilah discovered automatic writing quite by accident one morning while sitting at the breakfast table having her morning coffee. Bob had left for work and the children had not yet awakened. She was still half asleep while doodling on a note pad in front of her, when the pencil started to move on its own. Then the name Oliver came through, then the pen went on to say that he was being assigned to help her understand psychic relationships. The pen stopped writing. Ilah was amazed, she knew no one by that name and could not explain what happened. Then a couple of days later it happened again. The following is a letter I received from her shortly thereafter:

August 28, 1972

Dear Dick,
Thought you might enjoy reading this little gem that came through automatic writing last week. I swear I did not control it—but it is even hard for me to believe. The whole bit came through my *right* hand in about ten minutes' time, and I doubt that I could have consciously come up with some of this if I'd labored over it all day. I'll copy it just as it is, including the side comments.

"This is Oliver again. I was right-handed. We can go much faster now. Just relax and let me do the writing. You are wondering about many things. I will try to help you understand if you will clear your mind of preconceived ideas. Everything in the universe has power beyond your comprehension in your conscious state of mind. A molecule is the smallest form of matter. Each one contains energy cells as evidenced by the discovery of the atom bomb. Let me control the pen. You are too tense. Breathe deep and steady. Rid yourself of outside interference. Each living body consists of a mass of molecular energy. The brain is very complex in nature and does not die at any time. You must believe this to attain oneness with the one you worship. The brain is the seat of accumulated knowledge. Not all of it was learned in the present existence. You call it reincarnation, which in itself has some misconceptions. Do not denounce those who claim recall of prior lives. This is possible but is best understood by the small child, who does not communicate. A soul reborn is like a battery recharged. The energy is there to bring forth the knowledge stored in the reborn molecular matter. A child knows this but cannot communicate it. At an advanced age in his new existence the memory has been blocked out by the pressures of learning control of the physical body now harboring the soul. Do not put questions to me. I am only trying to help you understand. Be more patient, I am busy too. You will be confused unless you allow me to re-educate you. At one time you understood, as you were a philosopher with a quest for knowledge of the spiritual world not understood by your contemporaries. Get more paper. You wish answers to the question of a religious nature. Each life decides for itself. I cannot give you all the answers. I am searching too and must learn obedience before all things are revealed even to a soul held in abeyance. It is essential to earthbound souls to seek the mission of your existence and do what inner thoughts tell you is right. Do not be too influenced by the demands of society. Be alert to needs of contemporaries but not too self-sacrificing. Some exist only as a trial for the souls who are earthbound to find a more complete realization of their purpose for being. You are right to bring forth dream patterns. Your subconscious mind has access to the storehouse of knowledge within you. Many thoughts will be revealed to the alert brain whose physical body rests. Some is of no significance. It is only recall or revelation of future happenings. Your mind wanders. I will come later. Do not be discouraged. You have much to learn."

(End of automatic writing)

How about that? I think you'll agree that it doesn't really sound like the way I'd state it myself even if I tried. Parts of it don't really make sense to me—reference to the brain, for example. There was no punctuation, so I may have divided the sentences wrong in some cases. I was so spooked by this that I didn't try again for a couple of days and have had nothing but gibberish since.

Forgive, please, for bending your ear (or eyes . . . maybe). Just had to share this with someone besides Bob, and since I'm not in the mood to be carted off to the funny farm, you're my victim!

The rest of Ilah's letter was filled with family news, so I won't complete it. One of the more interesting aspects of the contact is that Ilah is left-handed. She can't write a thing with her right hand, yet on Oliver's instructions to change hands, she wrote easily. When in Minneapolis several weeks later, I saw the original writing. It was in bold, masculine penmanship, easy to read and exactly the opposite of Ilah's normal small, feminine script.

Dreams

There are many kinds of dreams and some are actually the memories of past lives, seen very much like they would in a regression. If you recall dreaming of yourself looking different than you do now, in period costumes, or in unfamiliar circumstances, you may be re-experiencing your own past.

These experiences can be intensified by asking to see the past, prior to going to sleep. Ask that it be revealed literally, and work at training your mind to remember immediately upon waking. Like other self-induced techniques, dream recall is a developed channel, dependent upon your own efforts.

Past-Life Circle

There are many unusual new individual and group techniques being developed to recall past lives. One, which seems quite successful, is the past-life circle. Dr. Gil E. Gilly, a fine psychic and good friend, uses this approach as part of his psychic development classes in Phoenix.

Gil acts as moderator, while the group sits in a circle. Breathing exercises and relaxation precede a technique of raising the consciousness to the higher-self level. Everyone in the circle then begins to "tune in." Verbal instructions to this effect are given:

"I am now receptive and ready to use any information about past lives to understand and improve my present life."

In talking with one of his students, I was told, "It always works . . . invariably someone will start picking up visual impressions, and before they can verbalize them, someone else will tap in on the pictures and begin to talk about it.'

When there is confusion or need of moderation, Gil uses his own psychic abilities to clarify the situation.

Questions About
Reincarnation

METAPHYSICS IS A SCIENCE/RELIGION/PHILOSOPHY OF self in relationship to the Universe. It is karma (cause and effect) and reincarnation.

Karma was discussed in the first chapter, and reincarnation is obviously the subject of the entire book. It is a practical, ethical, and logical code of absolute justice, directly affecting how you live your life. Hundreds of internationally famous people have publicly proclaimed their firm belief in reincarnation. Plato, Voltaire, Ludwig von Beethoven, Ralph Waldo Emerson, Victor Hugo, Henry David Thoreau, Jack London, H. G. Wells, Mark Twain, Louisa May Alcott, Henry Ford, and George S. Patton are but a few of those who have carried conscious memories of other existences or have accepted reincarnation as their philosophy of life. Often those unwilling to consider reincarnation a valid theory, worthy of consideration, have allowed their misconceptions about the subject to block all possible speculation or study.

When lecturing or performing group regressions, I always allow for a question-and-answer period. There are usually skeptics and nonbelievers present, and inevitably certain questions and challenges come up. The following are examples of the sort of questions most often asked. The answers are "my truths" based upon the regressions I've completed and nine years of intensive study and involvement with some of the country's leading psychics, mediums, astrologers, and metaphysical organizations.

Q. If we have lived before, why do we forget our past lives?

A. To handle the present and also remember all the past would be too overpowering for our present state of awareness to cope with. We ourselves have chosen this amnesia . . . we hope we have carried with us intuitive knowledge of what is right and wrong, so we do not make the same mistakes we have made in past lives. Everyone has strong feelings about certain things that cannot be traced back to any particular origin.

Q. How do you explain the population explosion?

A. There are simply more chances to be born now than at any other time in recorded history. There is no shortage of souls seeking the opportunity to advance themselves through earthly incarnations, only a shortage of bodies. The vibrational rate of today is higher than it has been within our "age," and thus it offers the chance for more rapid advancement than ever before.

Q. There are presently more people living on the earth than the sum total of all the people who have ever lived. Wouldn't this fact disprove reincarnation?

A. To begin, I don't know that this fact is true, in that general history would not include the past civilizations of Lemuria and Atlantis, and perhaps many others. This is really unimportant for it can be easily explained. There are many souls experiencing life on the earth plane for the first time. They may not have lived a physical existence before, or they may have lived within a different system (on another planet or within another dimension of time as we know it). Although I know of people within our country who are here for the first time, I personally believe that most first incarnations begin in more primitive or backward societies. Based upon the hypnotic regressions I have completed, at least ninety per cent of those in the United States have had lifetimes in Atlantis, which was a highly evolved society. We are back again because we function well in this accelerated frequency or vibration, which is similar to that of Atlantean times.

Another metaphysical theory, which is part of my own belief system, is the concept that an identity is capable of living several physical lives at the same time. In other words, one frequency of potential (soul) can occupy several bodies at once. Separate-selves seek to explore numerous potentials at the same time, during a period of accelerated vibrational opportunity. If this is the case, there are far fewer souls presently upon the earth than a census would confirm.

A good friend of mine feels she is also a nurse presently working in a hospital somewhere in this country. She has been drawn to and "merged" with a woman of totally different physical characteristics while experiencing an altered state of consciousness. My friend, Peggy, is an advocate of herbs and faith healing. While out of her body and in the hospital environment, she has observed the nurse's frustrations with the limitations of hospital procedures. Peggy has attempted to communicate mentally to her separate-self (the nurse) that there are more ways of healing than those endorsed by the AMA.

Enough substantial evidence has been provided to me through psychic channels to conclude that I am presently experiencing many potentials of physical and nonphysical existence. Investigation of the examples provided from the other side, of parallel incarnations, proved to be almost more than I was capable of perceiving. They also provided many valid explanations for various influences in my life, for each portion of the potential exploration (individual identity) intuitively influences the others.

Q. Why isn't there anything in the Bible about reincarnation?

A. Reincarnation was an essential part of the early Gospels, and its removal has never been fully accounted for. Evidence points to the fact that Emperor Justinian and Empress Theodosia (508–547 A.D.) deleted all reference to reincarnation from the then existing scriptures ... producing with their council the Bible that is accepted today. There is nothing in the Bible that contradicts reincarnation; in fact, there are many passages which allude to it, such as Jesus's own statement that John the Baptist was a reincarnation of Elijah:

Matthew 11: 13–15
> For all the prophets and the law prophesied until John.
> And if ye will receive it, this is Elias, which was for to come.
> He that hath ears to hear, let him hear.

Matthew 17: 10–13
> His disciples asked him, saying, Why then say the scribes that Elias must first come?
> And Jesus answered and said unto them, Elias truly shall first come, and restore all things.
> But I say unto you, that Elias is come already, and they knew him not, but have done unto him whatsoever they listed. Likewise shall also the Son of man suffer of them.
> Then the disciples understood that he spoke unto them of John the Baptist.

Here is another Biblical passage which seems to suggest reincarnation:

Revelation 3:12
> Him that overcometh will I make a pillar in the temple of my God, and he shall go no more out:

Q. I thought the Bridey Murphy story had been debunked?

A. When *The Search for Bridey Murphy* broke in the mid-1950s, it caused a nationwide interest in reincarnation. It was the first regression case to really be made public, and all attempts to debunk the story have failed. Time has actually filled in additional details that only strengthen it. A well-known Boston psychologist developed his own abilities in regressive hypnosis to disprove Bridey Murphy's story, and he wound up totally accepting it instead.

Q. Wouldn't the theory of reincarnation discount inherited qualities?

A. Inherited as you think of it, yes. But two artistic parents might very well have an artistic child. This doesn't mean the child actually inherited the qualities; it means that those parents would probably attract an artistic soul to be born through them. This would explain physical defects as well as attributes.

Q. When does a soul enter a baby's body?

A. At the time of birth. I often carry an individual forward in regression to the time of his birth in his present lifetime. The situation is always the same. For a long time prior to birth, he will be close to his parents-to-be . . . invisible to them, but constantly around them. "Learning to love them," are words I have often heard when asking, "Why are you there?" An interesting fact to me is that although an entity enters the baby's body at birth, it does not seem compelled to stay there while the baby is very young. It comes and goes. On several occasions I have asked someone what they were doing, and they have explained that they were out of the body, but nearby watching it. Another interesting thing to remember the next time you are with an infant is that the baby has all of the spiritual knowledge of the other side, and of the earth plane, and of you. He understands much more than you do and every word you say. He simply has no way to communicate with you. As he begins to develop, he loses his knowledge and awareness. By the time he can effectively communicate, except in rare cases, his past awareness is blocked from his conscious mind.

Q. Do you believe in God more, or less, after working in regressive hypnosis?

A. Much more. But not as a judging entity sitting on a throne in heaven. I believe that we are all God—all part of the whole. What one person does affects the whole. I see God as a form of energy gestalt. The metaphysical poet William Blake wrote, "Energy is eternal delight." We are all part of that total energy. Some of this energy has always been at a God level, creating souls, which, through experience and thus development of wisdom, would evolve back to the God level as a form of procreation and expansion, the universal goal being the eventual evolution of all energy to the highest level. God does not judge us. Through the universal law of karma (cause and effect) we judge ourselves. It is inescapable, and we, and we alone, are responsible for everything that happens to us.

Q. What about the Devil?

A. I do not believe in the devil, but I believe that those who do can actually create him. Thought form is every bit as real as the house you live in. In fact it is more real, as can be evidenced by regressive hypnosis. The house will someday fall into dust, but the thoughts of thousands of years ago can be recaptured.

Metaphysics as a philosophy would totally reject the idea of controlling people through fear. The devil is a fear-based idea, used by some religions to control their congregations. But ideas become reality. If you give them power, you can create a devil to the point of actually being able to conjure him up.

I do believe that there are negative forces that can effect us. These are primarily discarnate souls that are trapped on the lower astral planes. Some people would call them evil, but I would prefer to say that they are confused and unknowledgeable. Their own level of awareness keeps them trapped, and they often do harm without realizing it.

From my personal experience I can tell you what

transpired in our home. The house was built on an old gold mining claim. We had been aware for some time that we had an unseen visitor living with us, and in time he began to exert undesirable influences. Trenna has considerable psychic attunement and began to develop bad side aches which she could dispel by using the protectory device of mentally creating white light around herself. This proved the side aches were not physical manifestations. By putting her into a deep hypnotic trance, we were able to make contact with a miner who had been dead for more than one hundred years. Someone had hit him in the side with a shovel and he had died slowly, filled with hatred and bitterness. These negative emotions had held him earthbound, feeling the death pain and wandering around the area in a confused state of mind for all those years. I explained the situation to him, that he was actually dead and that he could let go of the pain and his present condition if he could only let go of the past. He had not realized that he had been transferring his pain to Trenna, and felt very sorry for having done so.

I was able to call in other, more highly evolved spirits to help him understand. They turned out to be his mother and an old Indian who had been close to him in life. Shortly thereafter they took him away, and we have experienced no further effects. We found out a couple of weeks later that one of our neighbors had actually seen the manifestation of an old miner in her kitchen on occasions prior to our own experiences.

Q. The theory of reincarnation is considered "metaphysical or occult thinking," and many churches condemn it.

A. I do not like the word "occult," for it denotes black magic in the minds of many people. In actuality occult means to conceal, but it has become synonymous with the supernatural.

Metaphysics explains what we call supernatural, but the philosophy does not encompass cults or unusual rituals. In reality there is no "supernatural," all is natural, there are simply some things beyond understanding within an earthbound perspective.

There have been those throughout history who have understood the secrets and powers of the Universe, but in other times this knowledge had to be concealed or kept secret for one's own safety. Even today this is esoteric knowledge. Metaphysically oriented people seldom attempt to convert others. They may explain and offer examples to substantiate the validity of their philosophy, but they also know that no one will be interested who isn't "ready."

I realize that many churches openly condemn metaphysics, and this is hard for me to understand, for it is a philosophy of justice and love. It is interesting, though, to note that the denominations that are most guilty of this base their recruiting techniques, printed propaganda, and services upon fear . . . damnation, hell, and the devil.

Q. You talk about absolute justice in Karma and reincarnation. Doesn't the same apply to Christianity?

A. Please don't get me wrong, I am not against Christianity. In fact I accept most aspects of it. Metaphysics is compatible with Christianity and Judaism. It does not negate the beliefs of these organized religions; it explains them. It goes beyond and looks at life from a larger perspective, above and beyond the physical view of man.

Some of the country's metaphysical leaders have been Christians who have maintained their religion, but broadened their views. Edgar Cayce and Jean Dixon are perfect examples.

I do absolutely reject fear as a tool of Christianity, and I find no justice within the accepted conceptions of heaven and hell. Established religions cannot explain the inequalities we constantly see around us.

Karma, being totally just, fully explains the supposed inequality. The church teaches that you will go to heaven or hell when you die. This says that there is a dividing line. If you are just good enough, you'll make it to heaven . . . a few degrees less and you go below. The metaphysical belief is that heaven and hell are of your own making. There are higher and lower planes on the other side. The lower are much less desirable; the higher are closer to God. Through reincarnations we return to learn on the earth and to advance our vibrational rate (level of consciousness) so that we may move closer to the perfected, or God level.

Q. Can we reincarnate as animals?

A. I have never found evidence of transmigration. Many metaphysically oriented people believe that souls evolve through the mineral, plant, and animal kingdoms. There are beliefs in group-animal souls. To me this is really unimportant. I do believe that animals reincarnate, and I could fill a book with stories to substantiate this belief. Love as a universal force is the energy which reunites souls on all levels.

One of my favorite stories is of a very warm woman I know who works as a psychic in Phoenix. She had a cat that was very close to her. During the readings the cat would come in, do a distinctive circle maneuver, and then jump up on her desk to sleep while her mistress talked with her clients. In time the cat was hit by a car and tossed into a wrought-iron fence, breaking its back. The vet was able to save its life, but from that time on the break, although completely healed, was obvious. Eventually the cat died, but within weeks the psychic's best friend's cat had kittens. One of the kittens had an out-of-joint backbone, which was caused by reincarnating too fast—carrying the physical defects from a prior life into the present life. Naturally the psychic immediately adopted the new kitten, who soon began to exercise the same circle maneuver before jumping upon the desk to sleep while her mistress worked.

Q. Where do you go when you die?

A. Immediately after death an entity will usually find itself right in the proximity of its dead body. Such entities, of course, are free of the body. When asked in regression how they feel, a very normal reaction is, "Light, I don't feel anything, I seem to be floating." They often are in a position of being above their body, looking down on it. Another reaction is an impression of intense light or warm color. Once in a while there is confusion, for they will not realize that they are dead. Sometimes there are other friendly entities there to guide them, and sometimes they appear shortly thereafter. Often an entity stays around to attend his own funeral.

When regressing someone, I will usually carry them to the last day of their life, find out what the situation is, then instruct them that they are going to go through the death experience as an observer, feeling no emotion or pain. Once they are in spirit, I will question them about what they are experiencing, and about the life they just completed—what they feel about what they accomplished.

I recently regressed a woman who was experiencing a male incarnation in the trance. Death occurred while he was drinking with several others; he just collapsed and died. From the spirit level, floating above the body, he showed considerable hostility toward the others, who thought he had simply passed out. He told me, "The fools don't realize I'm dead."

It is possible to follow an entity only a certain distance into spirit, in most cases. There is a point where they cease to be able to supply me with answers from the trance state. In time the departed soul will go to the level of his vibrational rate. This does not mean that he is not free, in his normally invisible spiritual body, to return, observe, help, and learn in the environment of the earth plane.

Q. What do you do between lifetimes?

A. You rest, work and learn in spirit just as you do on the earth plane. Often an entity will have to go back over his entire earthly lifetime, looking at it as if it were a movie, examining his mistakes and impressing them upon his consciousness so that when he returns he will use his intuitive knowledge not to make them again. He might work as a guide or helper to those on the earth or those trapped in the lower astral planes. On the other side you are without a body, but you still have your free will. No one will force you to do anything. You can goof off over there just as you can here . . . only you will keep yourself on the track of advancement. But in spirit you will be more aware of the true meaning of the goal, so it is more likely that you will work all the harder to achieve it.

Q. Do you change sexes and, if so, why?

A. Individuals seem to return predominantly in one gender, but they will always change sexes once in a while. To learn all that there is to learn, we must experience everything that is meaningful on the earth plane. Some of this knowledge could be attained only by changing sex. On the spiritual planes there is no gender, so in actuality we are all unisex—equally male and female. Many people involved in metaphysics believe that homosexuality is usually a case of an individual who has been a female for many lifetimes, changing sex and coming back as a male (or vice versa). The change is more than they are able to accept, due to the long history of subconscious programming as a female or male.

Q. The idea of living another life with my ex-husband is terrifying. Once is enough. Will I have to be reborn again?

A. This question is being asked from the extreme limitations of an earthbound perspective but, to answer it as best I can, I would say that no one will force you to be reborn but yourself. Many choose to experience within other dimensions of reality, never incarnating on the earth plane, although I've found that most souls, here now, are experiencing a rapid series of earthly reincarnations. How you look upon a situation from a spiritual or soul level may vary greatly from the way you see it from your present situation.

You and your ex-husband may be the closest of friends or part of a soul group on the other side. You may simply have decided to work together in this life on needed lessons for your soul's growth.

Q. If you find out through regressions that you did something wrong in a past life, wouldn't you feel guilty in the present?

A. I don't know of anyone who has. The past-life experience was obviously needed learning, which may have been a mistake from a karmic perspective, but it also may very well have already been balanced. Or you may have learned wisdom through the situation and thus would have risen above the necessity for future tests or balances.

Guilt is a negative fear-based emotion which, from my perspective, should never be accepted. Give it consideration only if you intend to remedy the situation . . . otherwise file it away labeled "experience."

If someone else attempts to make you feel guilty, they are either trying to control you or to hurt you. Neither situation is worth your consideration. There is an old metaphysical adage that is very apropos, "What other people do does not affect you . . . what you think about what they do affects you."

Q. If vocational patterns and abilities develop over several lifetimes, does this mean I'll be better at what I do now in my next life?

A. I have found continuing evidence through regression after regression of abilities developing over several lifetimes. In the area of music this could easily explain such cases as Chopin, whose concerto was publicly performed when he was nine years old, Beethoven, whose work was performed when he was eight, and Schubert, who composed at the age of eleven.

I feel there are good odds that you will be drawn back to the same work, lifetime after lifetime. The recall of your own past obviously offers you insight into professions for which you might have an affinity. This of course can show you the negative as well as the positive paths.

I remember having dinner with a good friend who is a professional singer and song writer in California. Although we agree on music, he felt my work in hypnotic regression was ridiculous. He did not believe he could be hypnotized and had absolutely no belief in reincarnation. Our dinner conversation turned to the subject of symbols, and he mentioned that he felt there was a symbol somewhere in his past that had great importance to him. He had attempted, unsuccessfully, to draw it on several occasions. I explained that he might be able to recapture it under hypnosis if he was willing to give it a try. He agreed, and as it worked out was a somnambulistic subject (the one person in ten who goes quickly to the deepest level of hypnosis).

Once he was in a deep trance, I instructed him to go back into his own past and draw a picture of the symbol. He drew a sword. I asked him the meaning of the symbol, and he said, "to kill." I asked him where he was, and he answered, "Rome."

The subject in this lifetime is greatly fascinated by guns and knives. He collects and treasures them and has repressed inclinations toward fighting. Several times he has considered becoming a mercenary in some obscure conflict.

Under regression it was revealed that he went through a lifetime as a Roman soldier and through the death experience as an old man. The next lifetime was that of a Spanish soldier during the Inquisition in Mexico—this time he died a slow and painful death while on a campaign. Each time I questioned him after he had crossed over into spirit, he felt remorse about the life he had just completed. The next incarnation was on a farm in Iowa, and he relived again, as an observer, a horrible death in 1918 in France during World War I. A karmic pattern of soldiering was obvious, and you couldn't ask for a more graphic example of "dying by the sword."

We also established another karmic pattern, in that music was part of his life during the Iowa incarnation. He played the mandolin at local socials with a group of musicians. He said, "I don't play very well." Today he plays the guitar—very well—and is quite successful in his musical career.

Q. I was very much attracted to this man, and we had an affair. If I knew him in a past life, could it be that I couldn't help what happened?

A. No. Free will is always a factor, but if you knew him in a previous existence, you were certainly far more drawn to him than you would have been if you had not had past ties. I couldn't start to draw a conclusion as to the karmic aspects of your affair. All the circumstances, actions, and reactions would come into play in an attempt to begin to judge the plus and minus karma resulting from the two of you getting together.

Q. How can you possibly justify divorce as part of your belief system?

A. Divorce in this country has become as common as the common cold, necessitating new pairings and new combinations of energy. I'm certainly not endorsing it, but I do not believe it is due to a loss of national morality, or to any of the judgments implied by the churches, psychologists, and behaviorists of the world.

Those now living have returned to experience the maximum potential within a minimum amount of time. To remain in a relationship that restricts growth is undesirable, and with new laws and the removal of social stigma, it has become a dispensable predicament.

Q. If I could understand through regression why my wife treats me the way she does, would I be able to accept her attitudes more easily?

A. You might, but regression isn't a magic wand. Often knowing the cause is a value in understanding the effect, but it doesn't change the present. Only you can do that

. . . and you must understand that you can change yourself, but you can't change anyone else. If you change, you will be, to a degree, another person, and this in itself may cause your wife to react to you differently.

Q. Can some people remember past lives on their own?

A. Yes, through an expanded awareness and learned or developed techniques, such as self-hypnosis, meditation, or dream interpretation. I know a man, who is a nationally known metaphysical author, who developed a technique of seeing his past lives, under certain conditions, in a mirror.

I have known individuals, who, without trying, have lapsed into a daydream-like trance and picked up involved past-life impressions. One of my closest friends has had this happen on several occasions. The last time it occurred he saw himself in a situation in early England. It made such an impression on him that he and his wife are currently planning a trip to that country.

Children, especially until they reach the age of about seven, will on occasion seem to be able to recall segments of past lives. When impressions come in, they express them very naturally, because to them they are natural and real. My brother and his wife live in the East and related a situation of taking their six-year-old daughter on a trip downtown. They went into an old building, and the little girl remarked, "I've been here before, Mommy." It was explained to her that she had not been in that building before. The child then explained, "Oh, not this time, I mean back when I was a big people."

Q. I've heard that many people who believe in reincarnation feel that time doesn't exist, that everything is happening right now.

A. I personally believe this, and science is coming to the conclusion that neither time nor space is real. The concept is that everything that has ever happened is happening right now, and that everything that will ever happen in the universe has already happened. In other words, that we are living all our lives, past, present, and future (so to speak), at this moment. There is only a constant "now." It is an oversoul concept that is quite hard for most people to perceive, but to me it really isn't important. We are here to experience, and our belief system is one of sequential time.

Q. Have you ever progressed anyone while under hypnosis into the future?

A. I have not, although I know of colleagues who have. Only time will prove the validity of what they have received. I personally am against it, for if a negative situation should be encountered I believe it could program the mind negatively. Negative thought, if dwelt upon, gives a negative idea power, and thus could be responsible for undesirable effects through self-creation at some time in the future.

The Mind Levels

"We use a maximum of five per cent of our mind.
Is it not comprehendible that a larger perspective is contained within the remaining ninety-five per cent?"

THERE ARE THREE MIND LEVELS: THE CONSCIOUS, THE subconscious, and the superconscious. Each level plays a different role in our lives.

Conscious Mind: will, reason, logic, and the five physical senses.
Subconscious Mind: imagination, memory, habit patterns, emotions, and the Akashic records.
Superconscious Mind: The creative force and psychic abilities, plus unlimited unknown powers.

We are all familiar with the general working of the conscious mind, but few people have an understanding of the subconscious. In addition to imagination, memory, and emotions, it is responsible for our habit patterns. These can be either positive or negative, and the negative habit patterns are often our hangups. The subconscious has little reasoning power. If improperly programmed in the past, it can work against the desires of your conscious mind in the present.

Negative subconscious programming does not necessarily come from your experiences in this life, but may very well have taken place in past lives. More often than not, regressive hypnosis shows that the fears being experienced in this life are due to a situation or series of situations that have taken place in a previous existence. To rise above these negative habit patterns (negative karma), we must re-program our subconscious mind. All hangups are rooted in fear. Fear is responsible for all mental disturbances, and to overcome fear programming we must replace it with positive programmings . . . love, peace, positive concepts and self-image. There are many ways to achieve this. Hypnosis, self-hypnosis, meditation, psychocybernetics, mind control, and premonstration are but a few, and they all overlap each other in actual practice.

The subconscious mind is also a complex storehouse of knowledge. From the metaphysical viewpoint of reincarnation, your subconscious mind carries the memories and influences of all your previous experiences. You are a sum total of all your lives. It explains your natural affinity for some things and your aversion to others.

As examples: The man who for no apparent reason is fearful of going out on the ocean in a boat may have drowned in the ocean in a past life. The natural artist who without training has drawn pictures well above average since he was a child has probably been an artist or involved in art-related areas in other times.

I know of the case of a woman with an intense aversion to perfume. She worked as a nurse in a doctor's office and would call all female patients before their appointments and ask them not to wear perfume into the office. This hangup was getting in the way of her work. Under regressive hypnosis, she saw herself in an Eskimo lifetime. She was being raped by a man who put his hand over her face while attempting to restrain her. His hands were covered with the strong smell of ambergris (a whale oil which is used in manufacturing perfume), and the experience had carried over into this lifetime in the form of an aversion to perfume.

In a recent case of mine we were searching through regression for the beginning of a problem between a woman and her stepson. The boy carried unwarranted hostilities toward her and several other family members. In regression she saw a heresy trial, which took place in Europe several hundred years ago. Her present stepson was the accused, and several of those sitting in judgment, including herself, were his present-day immediate family. Unknown to the boy, his attitudes in this life were often based on the subconscious resentments from another incarnation.

This theory offers an explanation for the existence of problems that cannot be traced back to a cause in this lifetime.

In the memory banks of the subconscious there is a record of everything that has ever happened to you . . . every thought, every action. These memory banks are sometimes called the Akashic records, and all your past lives are recorded within them.

"As a man thinketh in his heart, so is he." What we think of as the heart is actually the subconscious mind. If you think negatively, you'll receive negative . . . positive begets positive. You are generally aware of this in your daily life, but from a karmic perspective it is absolute.

Thoughts are things and they create karma . . . and karma must be balanced. All thoughts remain forever in your subconscious.

We use rationalization as a defense mechanism to fight psychological pain, and thus we reduce our own self-awareness . . . usually blaming others for the discomfort we have created ourselves. Instead of reducing the pain by rationalizing and blaming others, we should try to eliminate the causes, which are the negative thoughts themselves.

The superconscious mind is often referred to metaphysically as the higher self—the God self or the I AM I. It is the power behind creative drive and psychic abilities. It is also unlimited in power and wisdom. Every man has consummate genius within him. By opening the doors to the superconscious, you can do anything as long as you use the power in a positive way. Thus you have the ability to self-bestow your own happiness and success, develop your own psychic abilities, or achieve help and guidance beyond anything we can consciously imagine.

Within this higher-self level there is a larger, universal perspective that we must be aware of when we seek the truth. We judge from an earthbound perspective, based on logic, sequential time, and science. Earthbound perspective would claim heredity and environment determine our lives. Universal perspective would teach that you choose your parents and environment and time and place of birth for the purpose of the experiences and opportunities you would receive in that position . . . and that your life is determined by your past lives and your life from the time of your birth to the present.

If mankind could "know thyself" we would live in a world of cooperation, love, and wisdom.

The fact that you are now alive on this physical earth plane confirms that you want to advance yourself by experiencing and learning.

Think of the spiritual planes on the other side as a ladder down a well. Each rung of the ladder is on a different level. The bottom rungs are far less desirable; they are damp, dark, and cold. As you climb the ladder, the atmosphere becomes lighter and warmer. Your goal is to get to the top and climb out into a beautiful environment that is beyond anything our present and limited perspective can possibly imagine.

Different groups give this top level different names, such as Nirvana, the God level, the seventh level, or Satori 3. Spiritually you want to get there. To do so you must raise your level of consciousness and awareness, and this can be achieved more rapidly in the physical body than it can in spirit.

The lower levels are called the lower astral planes. These are very undesirable and similar to the classic conception of hell. Stories of hauntings and ghosts are actually cases of confused entities who have trapped themselves on the lower astral by their own level of consciousness. They have the ability to rise above their situation even on the other side, but it often takes them hundreds of earth years to realize this. In time they usually listen to the advice of more advanced entities, who are always willing to help. On numerous occasions while regressing someone into a past life, I have had my subject find himself on the lower astral. The reaction is always the same and is usually described as "dark, damp, and fearful." The fact that such subjects have been reborn on the earth plane shows that they worked their way out of the situation.

At the time of death you will cross over, leaving the physical body you are presently using for the expression of your thoughts, and again become the spiritual being you actually are. You will have a particular vibrational rate at this time. The vibrational rate will dictate your level on the other side. If there are seven upper astral levels and you have the vibrational rate for the third level, this is as high as you will be able to go. You would not be able to withstand the higher, more intense vibration on the fourth through the seventh levels.

What determines your vibrational rate? Your thoughts and thus your deeds on the earth plane will determine your level of consciousness and awareness. Your level of consciousness determines your vibrational rate.

You were born with a vibrational rate you established in the past. The way you live your life will determine whether you raise or lower it in the future. If you could truly change your way of thinking and your life today, your vibrational rate would be changed tomorrow. Love, positive thought, and serving or helping others would certainly raise your level of consciousness. Hate, negative thought, and hurting others mentally or physically would surely lower it.

Most people involved with metaphysics agree that it is possible to advance yourself fifteen or twenty lifetimes in the time you have left in this life if you choose to open the doors to a larger awareness. Men such as Gandhi and

Albert Schweitzer must certainly have advanced themselves many lifetimes in the time they spent here.

When Jesus, speaking about what men called miracles, said, "These things ye too shall do and more," He was saying that we all have the potential of being Masters. Subconsciously that is our goal. There are many Masters . . . there are many among us now on earth and many close to becoming Masters . . . close to achieving the highest spiritual level. They have advanced their vibrational rate to the point that it will no longer be necessary for them to return to the constant cycle of rebirth on this physical plane of existence, except to show others the pathway.

Love

"CAN YOU TELL ME IF THERE ARE OTHER LIFETIMES IN which the two of you have been together?"

"How many stars are there in the sky? How many drops of rain?" David Paladin's eloquent words are representative of many statements from regression subjects. "It's a never-ending song . . . we must be together."

A happily married young woman once answered this question with, "We have known a spectrum of experiences, and we will continue to create that which fulfills our needs."

Love in the physical world is the result of a union on the spiritual planes. It has always existed and it will continue to exist. Every identity is guided through repeated experiences until karmic accounts have been balanced and past mistakes have been solved to achieve a physical and spiritual alliance of unconditional love. Conflicts within a relationship are simply part of a learning process.

I sat visiting with Paladin in his studio recently. "How would you define love, David?"

"Love to me is the absence of fear," he responded. "I don't believe that good or evil exists. Simply love and fear."

I agree with him completely, for to me love is the energizing force of the universe, and fear is the only problem that exists in the universe. A perfect love knows no fear.

There are, of course, many who have achieved a life-long, loving relationship. Those who know "true love" consistently find joy in their alliance. I believe they will be born together again . . . and again. They will have problems until they have evolved beyond the need of earthly incarnations, but their troubles will not be with each other.

An aged couple in Mesa, Arizona, both in their seventies, have been happily married for more than fifty years. Their primary misfortune in this time has been poverty and the lack of the most basic comforts. They live without air-conditioning in an area where summer heat often reaches 120 degrees. A small old trailer has been home for longer than they can remember, and their vintage automobile hasn't functioned in years. Yet they're happy and do not complain. They are together and grateful for each other.

Rising above negative karma is a matter of rising above fear, in a love bonding or any other situation in life. The old couple in Mesa have obviously achieved a fearless mutual love in the past, and they have not feared the poverty of the present. If their plight were a karmic condition, they probably could have solved their money problems had they set their minds upon doing so. The fact that they did not is unimportant, for they've known happiness despite their circumstances and thus have learned wisdom. Their perfected love has given them strength to endure their trials.

Love does not die; it cannot die. It is not limited to the physical boundaries of time and space. The bond between a man and a woman will continue as an exploration of their combined potential throughout their spiritual voyage. Incompatibility, fighting, and divorce are only temporary setbacks, or learning experiences obviously necessary to achieve harmony, to overcome fear.

Tension, frustration, anxiety, indifference, guilt, insecurity, selfishness, inhibitions, possessiveness, sexual problems, boredom, and lack of fulfillment are emotions rooted in fear, as in any problem or disruption of any kind between human beings.

Sexual love, as most of us know it, is primarily possessiveness. Possessiveness and the insecurity it stems from are fear-based emotions.

Being totally idealistic, what would "real love" be like? To begin with, it could not be diminished by anything the other person said or did. Your love would not be dependent upon being loved. You would give freely, without any expectation of return. In an environment of "real love," you would allow total freedom to your mate, expecting no more than the other could give. You would love for what the other was. You would not expect your mate to change, to be something he or she was not. You would find joy in the other's happiness. To "really love" someone, you need to be complete within yourself, and without fear. You then will find joy in the positive aspects of your relationship and allow the negatives to simply flow past you, without affecting you.

Most of us are far from attaining true love. Even if we believe in it, it is sometimes hard to live it. But what a beautiful relationship this involved-detachment would be. By accepting and granting freedom, not out of indifference but out of tenderness and caring, a couple can overcome karma and evolve beyond the level of problems. Since you would no longer be affected by the problems, you would no longer have the problems. Karma would be balanced, and your own wisdom would have erased the need for further learning.

If fear is the problem, love is the answer. Universal love. The goal of everyone now living upon the earth is to rise above fear and learn love. Most are unaware of this fact, but it is the reason we are reborn, over and over. We all subconsciously seek love, and love's perfection. If we cannot remember what we have forgotten, we will be given another chance to find it, when we are together again.

ABOUT THE AUTHOR

Dick Sutphen is an author, hypnotist and seminar trainer. He developed innovative group hypnosis exploration techniques that are now being used internationally. His bestselling books, **You Were Born Again To Be Together, Past Lives, Future Loves** and **Unseen Influences** have become classic metaphysical/self-help titles (Simon and Schuster, Pocket Books).

Dick has appeared on many TV shows such as **Good Morning America.** In 1976, he conducted the first nationally-broadcast past-life regression on **Tom Snyder's NBC Tomorrow Show.** A 1¾-hour **David Susskind Show** was built around Dick's work and is still being rerun years later as one of the series' most popular programs. He has appeared on over 350 radio or television shows.

Dick is the author of over 32 books and more than 300 hypnosis, meditation and regressive hypnosis tapes. He has a 16-year background in psychic investigation and human-potential exploration that includes being the founder and former director of a hypnosis center in Scottsdale, Arizona. Today, he conducts his world-famous seminar trainings throughout the country. He publishes *Self-Help Update*, a free, quarterly publication that promotes mental, physical and philosophical self-sufficiency, and keeps the reader abreast of Dick's latest research and results.

Dick Sutphen currently maintains residences in Malibu, California, and Scottsdale, Arizona. The major part of his time is spent directing the corporate operations and writing.

For a complete listing of Dick's books and tapes, and to receive *Self-Help Update*, please write: The Sutphen Corporation, Box 38, Malibu, California 90265. Phone: 213/456-7361.